KW-221-896

Contents

"Spartina" is a group of four Lancashire authors, Dorothy Pilling, Mollie Thompson, Daphne Tibbitt and Diana Underwood. They would like to thank all those persons who have so willingly supplied information and without whose help this book would not have been possible. The front cover photograph of Carlisle Castle is by David Joy and the map on the back cover is by E. Gower. Illustrations in the text are by H. Pilling; the title page drawing is of a Romano–British cauldron at Tullie House Museum, Carlisle.

Introduction

LAKELAND contains a wealth of beauty with rugged hills, peaceful valleys, lakes and rivers. These we will leave for you, the reader, to explore and enjoy as you will. Here we tell you of those things and places passed without the realisation of the interest they contain. The legends are about people, and their stories passed down through the centuries. The castles, abbeys and great houses we mention are all open to the public. To some there is free access, others are open daily; for private houses appointments have to be made. Of the many hundreds of interesting and ancient churches in Lakeland, space allows us to include only a few. We will take you back in time to the Ice and Stone Ages, travelling forward again with the Romans and Normans, the Tudors and the Jacobites to the present day. See *where* they lived—in the castles and houses; and *how* they lived—in the museums, which show relics from all the ages. In the present, take part in the many sports and pastimes found in the area, enjoy the many annual events, and afterwards try a traditional recipe!

1: *Lakeland's Early History*

THE history of the Lake District must be counted from a time long before the Lakes existed—to a time when the gentler sloping sedimentary rocks were forced aside by the volcanic intrusions of igneous rock, lava and hardened ash-layers we now know as the Castle Head and Walla Crag area of Borrowdale. But it was glacier ice which made the Lake District what it is today, scouring and grinding its way across the land to form corries and steep-sided valleys. The lakes now occupy the hollows gouged out of the rock and today the surface waters of some lakes are dammed by moraines, the debris of melting glaciers.

One of the most striking reminders of this period is Borrowdale's Bouder Stone, an immense 2,000 ton boulder 60 feet long and 35 feet high. The advancing glacier must have swept this giant along as if it were a mere pebble, and left it balanced precariously on a narrow edge where it has rested for over half a million years. Over the next few thousand years, nature covered her bare rock surfaces, plants and animals took up residence and finally man made his advent. The rocks were now to be used; fashioned into tools by his awakening intelligence. In the Great Langdale area, on the scree slopes beneath Pike of Stickle, there is a "Stone Age Factory" as it has been aptly named. Here on the mountain side the axes were rough-cut and then probably taken to the coast where sandstone was available for the grinding and polishing process. Among the scree, thousands of fractured axe heads have been found, undoubtedly the "failures" rejected by the stone age craftsmen.

Rock slabs and piled stones being the most permanent of nature's building materials, they have marked the settlement of successive waves of pre-historic civilisation. On Birker Moor in Eskdale is Barnscar and the remains of beehive huts of the Bronze Age period, and on Birket Common near Mallerstang are Bronze Age cairns from which was unearthed an incense cup. At High Borrans in Longsleddale a heap of stones is all that remains of a British settlement; other sites are at Threlkeld near Keswick and at Lacra Hill near Millom. Since megaliths and stone circles are such a feature of the Lake District a separate section has been devoted to the subject.

Moving a little nearer to our own time we still find stone playing an important part in local life. On top of a small hill near Hesket-in-the-Forest there is a large stone platform with a hole in the middle through which grows a hawthorn tree. By tradition this is supposed to be the site of "Court Thorn" where tenant farmers assembled to air their grievances at the manorial court. And almost yesterday, relatively speaking, a boundary cairn was set up south of the village of Wythburn where the road crosses into Westmorland. This heap of stones is said to mark the site of a battle between the Saxon King, Edmund, and Dunmail, the last Cymric King of Cumbria. Though Dunmail was defeated his name lives on, for this cairn of stones is known as Dunmail Rise.

Other sites of interest

On **Carrick Fell** near Mosedale—a fortified British camp.

At **Castle Carrock,** Brampton area—earthworks and pit dwellings known as Halsteads. When the cairn was opened up the skeleton of a man with a drinking cup was found.

At **Longtown,** Solway area—a large earthwork called "Arthuret Knowes." This tree-covered mound is said to be the site of the Great Battle of Ardderyd in 573.

At **Newbiggin,** Penrith area—British earthworks.

At **Eamont Bridge,** Penrith area—a site known as "Arthur's Round Table" which is a flat area 300 feet in diameter surrounded by a dry moat. Its purpose is unknown but its name gives rise to speculation, particularly when one considers that the ruined Pendragon Castle also stands in the Lake Counties, for "Uther Pendragon" is supposed to have been King Arthur's father.

Megaliths and Stone Circles

THE Lake Counties are particularly rich in megaliths and stone circles. There are over fifteen sites, large and small, where these standing stones can still clearly be seen, and one wonders how many other sites existed but are now covered by the earth accumulation of the ages. Modern man is so far removed in time from the builders of these structures that he can do little but guess at the purposes for which they were built. We have assumed that they were pagan temples where blood sacrifices were performed; however, some recent research work carried out by Professor Alexander Thom may cause us to review our somewhat patronising conclusions concerning the civilisation of our remote ancestors.

Professor Thom's surveys of hundreds of stone circles, both in Britain and in Europe, reveal that each site adheres to an exact mathematical formula structured upon the "megalithic yard" of 2.72 feet. Many of these sites are not "circles" at all, but ovoids based on a knowledge of Pythagorean triangles—and yet they were built many centuries before the time of Pythagoras. This raises the

12 msc

P37531

LONDON BOROUGH OF LEWISHAM
LIBRARY SERVICE

Author

Title

METROPOLITAN
SPECIAL COLLECTION

Books or discs must be returned on or before the last date stamped on label or on
card in book pocket. Books or discs can be renewed by telephone, letter or personal
call unless required by another reader After library hours use the Ansafone
Service (01-698 7347). For hours of opening and charges see notices at the
above branch, but note that all lending departments close at 1 pm on Wednesday
and all libraries are closed on Sundays, Good Friday, Christmas Day, Bank Holidays
and Saturdays prior to Bank Holidays.

40p.

By the same authors:
LOOKING AT SOUTHERN LAKELAND
LOOKING AT NORTH LANCASHIRE
LOOKING AT CENTRAL LANCASHIRE
LOOKING AT SOUTH LANCASHIRE

Other Dalesman books on Lakeland:
AROUND ULLSWATER AND PENRITH
CARLISLE
CENTRAL LAKELAND
FOLK LORE OF THE LAKE COUNTIES
GHOSTS OF THE LAKE COUNTIES
GRANGE AND CARTMEL
GRASMERE AND THE WORDSWORTHS
THE JOHN PEEL STORY
KESWICK AND NORTHERN LAKELAND
LAKELAND COOKERY
LAKELAND THROUGH THE YEAR
LEGENDS OF THE LAKE COUNTIES
THEY CAME TO THE LAKES

Looking at
Northern Lakeland

by "Spartina"

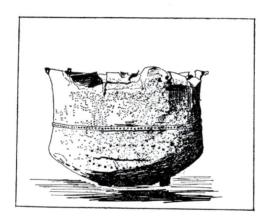

Dalesman Books
1972

The Dalesman Publishing Company Ltd.
Clapham (via Lancaster), Yorkshire

First published 1972

© Spartina 1972

ISBN: 0 85206 137 4

942.856

LEWISHAM LIBRARY SERVICE

LBN.	BRANCH	COPY
SBN.0·85206·137·4	12	
CLASS NUMBER 914·28	CATEGORY MSC	
BOOK-SELLER Bri	INVOICE DATE 2/11/72	
ACC. NUMBER	P 37531	

Printed by Galava Printing Co. Ltd.
Hallam Road, Nelson, Lancs.

interesting point as to the true level of culture of our ancient fore-
bears. Were the inhabitants of our islands that wise race of "Hyper-
boreans" spoken of with obvious reverence by the Greeks? And
were the megalith-builders really "astronomers" who constructed
their sites in order to make calculations concerning the movement of
sun and moon? Professor Thom is not alone in his views for other
archaeologists are investigating similar theories. To carry such
thoughts with us when visiting the Lakeland's stone circles surely
adds to that mysterious charm which has always surrounded these
ancient places.

Castlerigg

Route: Leaving Keswick, Castlerigg lies 1½ miles to the east.

Though smaller than the Little Salkeld site (see below), Castlerigg
Stone Circle makes an impressive sight standing on the plain high
above and to the east of Derwentwater. The site is termed a "circle"
but is in fact more oval in shape, 100 feet across and formed of 38
immense stones. Within this oval is an inner enclosure containing
10 stones.

Little Salkeld

*Route: Leave Penrith on A686; then on to secondary road for Little
Salkeld.*

"Long Meg and her Daughters" has been called Cumberland's
Stonehenge since it is the second largest stone circle in England. It
is 400 yards in circumference and contains 59 stones in all; some are
now level with the ground while the others stand erect around the
perimeter and many have a girth exceeding 15 feet. Of the types of
rock represented, greenstone, limestone and granite form the major
part. Long Meg herself stands alone several yards away from the
circle, a tapering and rather hunchbacked stone 18 feet high and
15 feet around with a possible weight of about 17 tons. Facing Long
Meg, a slight distance away, stand her four "daughters"—together
they seem to form a gateway entrance to the main site.

Standing Stones and Lesser Stone Circles

At **Distington,** north of Whitehaven off A596—small stone circle.

Near Setmurthy, on **Elva Hill** above Bassenthwaite Lake—a circle
of 12 stones, about 100 feet across. The stones are still visible, though
deeply sunken into the ground.

Penrith area: Near Mosedale, on the lower slopes of **Carrick Fell**—
small stone circle. Near Eamont Bridge, **Mayburgh**—an embankment
of earth and river cobbles above which stands one ancient stone,
9 feet high and 18 feet thick. It is known that at one time there were

eight standing stones on this site but this monolith is all that now remains.

The Romans

AFTER the invasion of England in A.D. 43, the Romans pushed steadily northwards and by A.D. 71 they occupied the Pennine area. About ten years later the governor Julius Agricola penetrated as far as southern Scotland but by A.D. 122 these Scottish conquests had been abandoned and, under orders from Emperor Hadrian, work began on a continuous line of fortifications stretching between Newcastle and Bowness-on-Solway. Hadrian's Wall then marked the northernmost limit of the Roman Empire. However, Hadrian's successor Emperor Antoninus Pius extended the frontier as far as the Forth/Clyde line—a barrier known as the Antonine Wall. From A.D. 139 until the Romans withdrew from Britain, the boundary line fluctuated many times between the Hadrian and Antonine Walls.

The Building of the Wall

ALONG the entire 73 mile length of the Wall at mile intervals were small forts or "milecastles," and between each pair were two turrets which served as signal towers. The milecastles varied slightly in design but the basic features were constant: they covered an area of about 60 × 75 feet with a north and south gateway, and barracks large enough to accommodate 25 to 50 men. The turrets were 20 feet square towers recessed into the Wall, with an upper storey level with the parapet-walk, and reached by an internal ladder. On the northern side of the Wall a great ditch or "Fosse" was dug and on the southern side a flat bottomed ditch or "Vallum" with earth ramparts on either side. Between the Wall and the Vallum was a road some 20 feet wide known as the Military Way.

The height of the Wall was some 15 feet with a parapet of six feet on top of that; the width varies in places from eight to ten feet.

The large forts vary in size and position depending upon the strength of the garrisoned unit. Some were built astride the Wall while others were quite a distance away. Rectangular in shape they had four "porta" or gateways, and streets leading to the "principia" or H.Q. buildings and to barracks, workshops, granaries, hospital, bath-house and stables if necessary. Petriana at Stanwix, Carlisle, was one of the larger of these forts; it covered $9\frac{1}{4}$ acres and garrisoned a cavalry regiment 1,000 strong. The defence scheme also extended northward beyond the Wall to such outpost garrisons as Banna (Bewcastle), and down the 40 miles of Cumberland coastline with a series of small forts, milefortlets and watchtowers.

The Wall Today

BEGINNING at Bowness-on-Solway, on the headland overlooking the Firth, is the site of a large fort with part of the ramparts visible. Built into a wall in the village is a tablet of the 3rd cohort of the 2nd Augustan Legion; in a roadside barn wall is a small inscribed altar and also in the village are traces of the Roman guard-room. Drumburgh (Congavata) was one of the smallest stations on the Wall; now only a few mounds remain.

From Burgh-by-Sands (Aballava) we move on to the fort at Stanwix (Petriana) which is now part of Carlisle. The camp at Carlisle (Luguvalium) existed before the Wall which, when it and Petriana were built, left Luguvalium as a civil settlement. Fragments of the ancient city can be seen in excavations within the grounds of Tullie House Museum. This museum exhibits a remarkably comprehensive selection of Roman antiquities found throughout the area.

North-eastward across country the Vallum is still visible in a number of places. Near Walton, Castlesteads (Uxellodunum) is the next site and here are small sections of Wall and the remains of a tower. On the site of the camp several figures and altars were dug up and they now stand in a garden setting. Three areas of the Wall still in a good state of preservation are Banks East Turret, Leahill Turret just beyond Lanercost and east of that, Piper Sike Turret.

Birdoswald (Camboganna) was the site of a large fort on the steep cliffs above the river Irthing. Still visible are parts of a dry ditch, sections of Wall six feet high and five feet thick and remains of a kiln used for drying corn. Nearby at Gait Crags is the quarry used by the Romans and some of the rocks still bear weatherworn inscriptions. Further along is the milecastle at Harrows Scar and from here are good stretches of Wall from Willowford Bridge to Gilsland, where there is the Poltross Burn milecastle. Through present-day Gilsland runs the boundary between Cumberland and Northumberland: but those interested in following the Wall eastward will find well over seventeen more sites between here and Wallsend-on-Tyne.

Inland and Coastal Forts

MANY of the soldiers who manned the forts of Britain were not full Roman citizens but recruits drawn from all over occupied Europe, and later many Britons were enlisted. Their wives and families as well as traders formed civil settlements in the locality of the forts and along the main routes which connected them. The Ordnance Survey Map of Roman Britain shows the extensive network of roads throughout the country.

First we will trace the main north/south route starting from Carlisle down through Wreay and on to Old Penrith (Voreda) which is now called Plumpton Wall. The outline of the fort ramparts and

stones from one of the gates are still visible. Roman altars carved
with figures were also found here. The A6 coincides with the Roman
road in many places, going past Salkeld Gate and down to Brougham
(Brocavum) where the Roman road forks south-eastward—the
modern A66. When the Penrith motorway was under construction a
large number of stone-lined graves and earthenware pots were uncovered on the site of a Roman burial ground. Kirkby Thore
(Bravoniacum) was the next large fort and here altars, ornaments and
coins have been found. The Roman road continues to Brough
(Verterae) and across to Catterick in Yorkshire.

Again starting from Carlisle we follow the route west across
country to the coast; the A595 is its modern equivalent. The fort of
Olenacum is in the Wigton area and has been called Old Carlisle.
Further south at Torpenhow, carved Roman stones can be seen built
into the church and these probably came from the small fort on
Caermote Hill. From Papcastle (Derventio) which is about a mile
from Cockermouth the road leads to the coastal fort near Workington (Gabrocentum). Here we join the Roman coastal road which
started from Moresby (Tunnocelum) and ran northward to Hadrian's
Wall. At intervals along this coastline there would have been small
watchtowers and beacons, but the next large fort was Maryport
(Alava). From there they continued to Beckfoot (Bibra) and across
the Waver/Wampool estuary to Bowness-on-Solway.

The Norsemen

OVER a thousand years ago the Vikings had already established
settlements in Ireland and on the Isle of Man, and it is more than
likely that the invasion of Cumbria stemmed from these outposts of
the Norse empire. Landing on our western shores they probably
engaged in short skirmishes with the local inhabitants before moving
up into the fells, a land whose topography must have reminded them
of their Scandinavian homeland. The independent farming communities set up by the Vikings lived on in the same pattern until quite
recently as the Cumbrian "statesman" or estateman. The practice of
dry-stone walling, and the dalesman's enjoyment of country sports
and wrestling are yet more reminders of the Norse way of life; in fact
very few areas of England carry such a clearly defined Norse heritage
as do the Lake Counties.

Some have said that even the dialect and physical appearance of
the dalesman bears striking resemblance to the Scandinavian, but the
strongest traces of the old Norse dialect remain in the words and place
names: "thwaite" a clearing, "fell" a hill, "thorp" a hamlet, "beck"
and "tarn" a road, "by" a village, "ghyll" and "slack" a valley.
However, since the invaders had arrived via Ireland they had adopted
many Celtic habits of speech. Aspatria was formerly Ascpatric or
Patrick's ash-tree, Setmurthey was Murdac's shieling and Brigsteer

was Styr's bridge; in each case the compound word reversed the
order of the personal name, a Celtic rather than Norse word-form,
whereas the first element of the compound is Scandinavian.

The invaders also brought with them their beliefs and traditions
and they have left permanent reminders built into the landscape.
Examples of the typical Viking hogback tombstones can still be seen
as part of the north wall of Appleby church, another near the church
at Aspatria, and a third at Plumland near Aspatria. In the churchyard at Dearham, near Maryport, there is a stone cross on which is
carved Yggdrasil of Norse mythology, the great Ash Tree which
supports the Universe. At Gosforth on the A595 north of Ravenglass
is a similar cross which stands near the lychgate of Gosforth church.
It is one of the tallest ancient crosses in England, fifteen feet high and
with a tapering shaft at the top of which is a four-holed head carved
with the triquetra, the emblem of the trinity. From the scenes
depicted on the four-sided column it would seem that those who
carved it were asserting that the new faith of Christianity would
triumph over paganism. Loki's wife and Odin's son are represented,
and also parts of a 10th century poem known as Vduspa or the
Sibyl's Prophecy.

The Fishing Stone, also at Gosforth church, reinforces the same
theme. The top panel shows a Holy Lamb trampling upon the
serpents of paganism and a further scene illustrates the story of the
god Thor fishing for the World Serpent; with Hymir he sits in a boat
fishing with a pole baited with a whole ox-head.

Viking hoards of weapons and plunder have been unearthed in
many areas of the Lake Counties. A hundred years ago, when the
lake at Kentmere was drained, the lake-bed revealed rich deposits of
diatomaceous earth in which were preserved Viking spearheads and
an oak dugout canoe. In the old forest of Inglewood, above Penrith,
is the village of Hesket-in-the-Forest and here it is said that a vast
hoard of richly decorated weapons was found beneath a mound of
earth. Regrettably no one knows what became of this treasure, but
with the Ormside finds we are more fortunate. The village of Great
Ormside, near A66 south of Appleby, is known to be the site of a
Viking settlement once called Ormshed, the seat of Orm the Viking.
Here a knife, a broken sword and the umbo or boss of a shield were
found and they are now exhibited at Tullie House Museum, Carlisle.
Perhaps the Ormside Cup was the most exciting find; a gold and
silver cup $5\frac{1}{2}$ inches in diameter set with gems. This is now in the
York Museum, a fitting place since York was another northern
Viking stronghold under Sihtric the One Eyed, a colourful character.

The Border Freebooters

DURING the days of the border fights between the English and
the Scots, the range of mountains between the warring factions
was often the setting for fierce and bloody battles. The two parties
were so hostile that there were no feelings of honour or obligation
between them. The border clans made frequent raids, plundering
cattle and property, and soon became known as "freebooters" for
eventually raids were made indiscriminately both on their rivals and
even on their own neighbours. Occasionally there were instances of
chivalry or romantic feeling in these battles, but these were rare when
lives were ruled by the sword.

The legend concerns a desperate battle between two rival clans of
the border freebooters, fought among the towering mountains of
northern Lakeland. Late one evening a party of men from the
English side of the border, weary after much fighting, were summoned
together by the sounding of their war cry. Scouts who had been
despatched in different directions to give warning of any impending
attack, returned to their chief, who sat by the watch fire on a neighbouring mountain, and told him that they had seen an invading
Scottish clan driving before them a large herd of stolen cattle. The
invaders had previously divided into small groups to travel through
the mountains, thus avoiding detection by the sentries posted throughout the district. They had plundered and pillaged as they had gone,
finally uniting again with their spoils. Again they had divided, this
time into two groups, one to drive the cattle towards the border, the
other to remain behind to cover their retreat. As the English war cry
rang round the mountains the Cumberland men gathered, each one
mounted on his small horse, called a pricker. These small horses were
both fleet and sure of foot, and well able to climb the rough mountains.

The Scottish freebooters were led by the Graemes who had stolen
and robbed as far south as Borrowdale, at the time considered a great
feat. The younger Graeme was a bold fearless warrior, and his father
Ossian inspired the young men with confidence by telling them tales
of his own past battles. When the rearguard troops had diverted the
English from following and regaining their stolen cattle, the clan

separated among the mountains to wait for the signal to attack, when they would rush down upon the Cumberland men. The English borderers, having been thwarted in their attempt to regain their stolen cattle, decided to seek their revenge on the Scottish side of the border. They gathered together their men and set off northwards through the wild and lonely mountains.

Information that the enemy was approaching was quickly sent to the young Graeme and the Highlanders crowded round their leader. The Scottish chief decided to wait until the enemy was trapped in a valley between two high crags before he attacked, and so the Highlanders hid themselves and waited. Soon the Englishmen approached the crags until they were opposite the ambush. Then the young Graeme stood up and waved his large sword towards the enemy. A volley of shots from the hidden troops followed. The elder Graeme aimed his musket at the English leader and killed him outright. At this, the English turned and furiously fired at the mountainside where the Highlanders had lain in wait. The young Graeme and several of his clan fell dead and the English, realising that this was a battle they would not win and still intent on their revenge, fled towards the border. The Scottish borderers were left mourning the loss of their leader, and the old chieftain wept as his son was laid in an opening in the mountainside. Every member of his clan laid a stone as a memorial, and finally on top of the pile they sorrowfully placed their dead leader's bonnet, shield and sword.

The Druid's Circle

JUST outside Keswick stands Castlerigg Stone Circle, thought to have been a Druidical Temple, where ancient man worshipped and offered sacrifices to his Deity. It is the setting for a legend about a young girl called Ella, and Mudor, the youth who loved her.

A mighty warrior once travelled northwards with a large band of followers until they reached a river at the foot of a tree-covered hill. Here they camped, making rough dwellings from branches covered with sods of grass. They hunted the wild deer in the forests, fished in the rivers, and their numbers grew. Their priests now moved to a quiet place among the mountains where the mistletoe, their sacred emblem, grew and there were plenty of stones to build their temple.

In the town at this time there lived a youth who was renowned for his great strength and his marksmanship with a bow and arrow when hunting. His name was Mudor and he was devoted to a young maiden called Ella. While they were still young they went to a place further up the river where a statue to the God Mogan stood. Before this image Mudor and Ella pledged their love, staining a blue sun on their breasts as a sign that their love would last as long as the light from the sun. They lived just outside the town in two adjoining cabins and they were blissfully happy. When Mudor returned from hunting

Ella greeted him warmly, and for her, Mudor made a coat of squirrel skins to keep her warm.

One day a fever broke out in the town and many people died. The inhabitants appealed to the priest of Mogan to spare them from the terrible disease, but the priest told them that this was a punishment for their wickedness. Then the Druids journeyed to one of their temples in the mountains. The Arch Druid gathered some mistletoe and when the sun rose he licked the dew from the berries and performed rituals that would tell him in what way he could appease the Great Spirit. He then claimed the answer was that they must sacrifice a young virgin. When they returned to the town with this news everyone was dismayed and all the young girls were afraid. The Druids gathered together and drew lots, and announced that the victim was to be Ella. Mudor was dismayed and begged the Druids to choose another victim, but the priests told him that they could not revoke the will of the Deity. Ella, however, accepted the decision calmly, her only regret being that she could not keep her vows to Mudor.

At last the morning arrived for Ella's sacrifice and she was taken out of the town. Mudor followed the procession of Druids and townspeople till they reached a place surrounded by mountains. The priests moved to the north side of a circle of stones which stood at this place. Then a small basket-work cabin was built and put by the circle. Into this the fair Ella was placed, wearing a garland of oak leaves and carrying mistletoe. After a sacrificial hymn to the sun had been chanted, dry leaves and small branches were put round the cabin. Everyone present had to place one stick in the sacrificial fire, but Mudor felt he could not take part in any way in the death of his beloved Ella. The Arch Druid then took two pieces of wood and rubbed them together till they were alight, then set fire to the cabin. The priests continued chanting as the cabin blazed, but suddenly they screamed in terror for a flood of water rushed from the rock, down the dell. The fire round the cabin disappeared and Ella emerged unhurt, to the joy of Mudor. The Arch Druid said that this was a sign that no more human sacrifices would be made. Ella and Mudor lived happily together to a great age, and it is said that from time to time the rocks in the dell still pour forth water.

John Peel

JOHN PEEL was born in 1777 at a cottage at Park End Farm just outside Caldbeck, and when he was only a few weeks old his parents moved to Greenrigg. He was baptised at the church at Caldbeck on the 24th September, the eldest of thirteen children. In 1797 he eloped to Gretna Green with Mary White, the eighteen-year-old daughter of a prosperous farmer from Uldale. They were married by the blacksmith at daybreak, but later at the request of Mary's parents, they were married again in Caldbeck church. He and Mary moved to a farm at Upton, Caldbeck, in 1803 and he lived and hunted all his life here and at Ruthwaite in the Caldbeck district, which is known as "Back o' Skidda."

Peel was 22 when he started hunting his own pack of hounds. Some of his hounds were kennelled at his farm, and the remainder were kept at neighbouring farms. At daybreak Peel would go outside and loudly blow on his hunting horn (this was the origin of one of the lines of the song). Then the hounds would converge on Peel's farm from all directions, eager and ready for the day's hunting. Peel lived for his hounds, to the detriment of his wife and farm. John and Mary had thirteen children, seven sons and six daughters, but nothing was more important to Peel than his hounds. Legend has it that even on the day Peter his son died, Peel was out hunting. A fox was killed and Peel had the fox's brush put in his son's coffin.

Peel himself was a tall, uncouth, hard-drinking, hasty-tempered and aggressive man both in manner and speech. For hunting he wore a long grey coarse woven Herdwick coat which came down to his knees, corduroy knee breeches and stockings, and a tall and rather battered light-coloured beaver hat. On the lower fells he rode a pony, a roan Galloway called Dunny, which was a cross between a fell pony and a cob. After a long day's hunting, Dunny would wait patiently for Peel while he spent many hours drinking and boasting of the number of foxes he had killed. Often Peel's clothes dried on him as he sat before the roaring log fire—for the huntsman, pneumonia was an occupational disease. At last Peel would be put on to Dunny's back and taken home, to be up again at the crack of dawn the following day. Sometimes he would walk as far as 40 miles over the rough fells, and his most famous hunt lasted for 70 miles and took his hounds through eleven parishes.

Often Peel would spend the entire night drinking, boasting and singing bawdy songs. It was during one of these evenings that he sat with his great friend, John Woodcock Graves, who came from Wigton but settled in Caldbeck and was a great admirer of Peel. As they sat by the fire one snowy night Graves began to scribble down the lines of a song. He wrote it of course in Cumberland dialect, not as it is sung today: "Did you ken John Peel wie his cwote sae grey?"

As Graves sat writing, a woman in the corner of the room was singing an old song called "Cannie Annie" to a baby she was nursing to sleep. When Graves sang his song to this tune, Peel is said to have listened with tears in his eyes. Later in 1868 a new tune was composed by Mr. William Metcalfe, the organist at Carlisle cathedral. With the new tune the song gained in popularity, thus immortalising Peel's name.

When Peel died in 1854, at the age of 78, his pack of hounds was disbanded. Some went to the Blencathra, which was being formed by John Crozier, the Squire of Threlkeld. These hounds were used for breeding, later generations eventually forming the present pack. Peel was buried in the churchyard at Caldbeck. As the coffin passed by Peel's cottage his hounds could be heard howling mournfully. His grave is marked by a white headstone, easy to find at the end of a well-worn path (see Caldbeck Church, page 45).

The Legend of Emma

THE original setting of this old Lakeland legend is not known, and the story itself gives no indication of where it might have taken place. The story concerns a young girl called Emma, who lived with her mother and father and enjoyed a very comfortable life. When her father died insolvent, Emma and her widowed mother were left almost destitute. Their only income was thirty pounds a year, and rather than deprive her elderly mother of the comforts she had become accustomed to, Emma decided to become a servant. Her mother strongly opposed this idea and threatened to beg, borrow or steal enough money to keep them both rather than allow her beautiful daughter to enter service. Emma was adamant, and the more her mother pleaded with her the more determined she became.

Eventually Emma obtained a position with a gentleman's family with whom her father had been friendly. The day came for Emma to leave, the first time she had been away from her mother, and their parting caused them both much unhappiness. Emma's mother sent her with her blessing, and Emma assured her that if any difficulties arose she would return home immediately, and she promised to write many letters.

Time passed and Emma, as she had promised, wrote long letters to her mother that she was well and happy—a fact confirmed by her mistress who also wrote. Then one day a letter arrived from Emma to say that she would be coming home on Whit Sunday morning to spend a week with her mother. The morning dawned clear and fine and Emma felt joyful as she gathered together her few belongings and the wages she had carefully saved before setting off on the journey home. The road led through a deep valley with overhanging trees on either side, and through the wood on one side ran a stream which fell as a waterfall over the rocks. The noise of this little waterfall could be heard for a considerable distance in the quiet wood. Where the stream left the trees there was a large rock which looked rather like a ruined castle, and at the foot of this rock, in the shade of an old oak tree Emma sat down to rest.

Unknown to Emma she was not alone in this romantic spot. Sam, a youth who worked as a cow hand at her master's farm, knew that Emma had received her wages and that she was now going to see her mother. Knowing which road she would take, Sam had taken a short cut across the hills, planning to rob her at this lonely place. As Emma sat resting, Sam suddenly appeared and demanded that she hand over her wages. Although Emma pleaded with him to leave some of her money as a present for her mother, the youth refused. Sam departed and Emma prepared to resume her journey home. As he left, Sam suddenly realised that Emma would name him as her assailant and he would doubtless be punished. There was only one thing to do. He returned to the glade and brutally murdered the poor girl leaving her body by the stream before fleeing for his life, never to be heard of again.

Meanwhile, Emma's mother became more and more concerned at the absence of her daughter. At last she could wait no longer and set out to meet her, having a premonition that all was not well. As dusk fell she reached the wooded glade, quiet except for the chattering of the waterfall, and there on the green grass lay the body of her beloved daughter, Emma.

The Legend of St. Cuthbert

ST. CUTHBERT was born in Northumbria about the year A.D. 635. Nothing more is known of his life until much later when he became a novice, under Abbot Eata, in the Abbey of Melrose, and after a time, Prior of Melrose. In 664 he went as Prior to Lindisfarne and remained there for twelve years before going to St. Cuthbert's Island where he lived the life of a recluse. He later moved to a remote island called Farne, and while he was living there he built his own chapel and was visited by the monks of Lindisfarne. In 684 he became Bishop of Hexham and in 685 the Bishop of Lindisfarne. During this time he travelled to many parts of the Lake Counties, including Carlisle. Once each year he visited St. Herbert, a Saxon priest who lived a life of prayer and meditation on a wooded island on Derwentwater. So close was their friendship that Herbert prayed they might both die on the same day and at the same hour—a prayer which was granted in 687. Before he died St. Cuthbert told his followers that God would show them where he was to be buried.

The next Bishop of Lindisfarne was Eadfrith who was an artist and is said to have written out the four Gospels. These were bound with metal work and precious stones and became known as the Lindisfarne Gospels.

Eleven years after St. Cuthbert died the monks decided to place his remains in a new monument. When his coffin was opened they found that his body and clothes were perfectly preserved and he looked like a man asleep. A picture of this can be found in Carlisle Cathedral. The body of St. Cuthbert remained at Lindisfarne till 875 when the Danes invaded the east coast. Bishop Eadred, seven priors and monks fled from the coast carrying the body of St. Cuthbert and the Lindisfarne Gospels. They also carried the preserved head of Oswald, King of Northumbria who was slain in battle in the year 642. According to tradition his head was later placed in St. Cuthbert's coffin as a holy relic. The monks travelled through the Lake Counties and as far south as Manchester before returning to St. Bees. Here they were again threatened by the Danes and they fled to Lorton before finally reaching Workington. Deciding that there would be no peace in England the monks decided to flee to Ireland. The ship set sail, but a fierce storm blew up, the sea appeared to turn to blood, and the precious Lindisfarne Gospels were washed overboard. The monks took this as a sign that they must remain in England and so they returned to the shore. The next night a vision of St. Cuthbert told them to search for the Gospels further along the coast. When the monks went to look they found that the sea had receded three miles and the Gospels were safe on the shore. They are now in the British Museum, still bearing salt stains from the sea.

In 955 the vehicle carrying the saint's body became stuck on its way from Ripon to Chester-le-Street. In a vision, one of the monks was instructed that the Saint's body must be taken to Durham. When they tried to turn round the next day the vehicle moved easily, and they travelled to Durham where St. Cuthbert was buried and the Cathedral was founded. When Durham Cathedral was plundered of its treasures in 1542 the monks hid the body of the Saint, the secret of the exact spot being handed down to the Benedictine monks.

During his life-time St. Cuthbert is said to have had a tumour of the breast which healed towards the end of his life. Some years ago the coffin of St. Cuthbert was opened and was found to contain the greater part of one skeleton and two skulls. One of the skulls had been severed by a blow with a sword or axe and was thought to be that of St. Oswald. The skeleton had a hole in the breast where there had been a tumour which experts claimed had been healing before death. This skeleton was claimed to be St. Cuthbert.

Mary of Buttermere

MARY ROBINSON was the beautiful daughter of the inn keeper of the **Fish Inn** at Buttermere. Although she was unknown outside the valley, locally she was renowned for her outstanding beauty. However, when she married, she suddenly found herself a celebrity, and Coleridge, Southey and Wordsworth all helped to make her name known throughout the country. It was in 1802 that Mary fell in love with a stranger who came to stay at her father's inn. She was a girl of 18, while he was 44 with a past of which she knew nothing. The stranger was John Hatfield and he was one of the most outrageous imposters of his time.

John Hatfield was born in 1759 of poor parents in Mottram, Cheshire. Here he spent his childhood and early manhood before beginning work as a traveller to a draper in the north of England. His first marriage in 1771 was to a daughter of Lord Robert Manners who, believing him to have a promising future in the business, gave him as a wedding present the sum of £1,500. When this money had been squandered in London, Hatfield left his three children and his wife, who later died of grief. By now he had acquired the name of "Lying Hatfield."

After this Hatfield lived by claiming to be a member of the family of the Duke of Rutland, but was imprisoned for a debt of £160. Somehow he managed to convince a clergyman, who was visiting the prison, of his innocence; the clergyman in turn persuaded the Duke of Rutland to pay his debts and give him money. Soon Hatfield had squandered this money as well and was imprisoned again, after living as an imposter both in Ireland and Scarborough. In prison in London he managed to make contact with a Miss Nation, from Devonshire, who lived opposite the prison with her mother. Although she never actually met John Hatfield, she paid his debts and when he was released they were married. They went to live in Devonshire, where he persuaded some respectable merchants to take him into partnership. Suspicions as to his character and money arose and so he fled, abandoning his second wife and two young children at Tiverton.

This time he fled to Keswick, where he arrived at the **Queen's Head Hotel** in 1802, in grand style complete with carriage and horses. He now took the name of the Hon. Alexander Augustus Hope, the brother of the Earl of Hopetoun, Member of Parliament for Linlithgow. Again he lived by fraud and forgery and it was here that he heard stories of the beautiful Mary. Although at this time he was courting a wealthy lady in Keswick, he decided to visit the **Fish Inn** and see for himself the Beauty of Buttermere. He arrived under the name of The Hon. Col. Hope, and Mary, who soon succumbed to his flattery, found herself in love with the charming stranger. His plans for marriage with the wealthy lady in Keswick came to naught so Hatfield pursued Mary in earnest. His past was never queried in the small hamlet and he and Mary were married in the church at Lorton in October, 1802. Mary's happiness did not last long, for Hatfield was challenged by a judge who knew the brother of Lord Hopetoun, and a warrant was issued by Sir Frederick Vane stating that Hatfield had forged letters as the Member of Parliament for Linlithgow. Hatfield was arrested, but escaped and after spending some time on board a ship at Ravenglass he went by coach to Ulverston and then to Chester.

As well as ruining Mary's reputation, he had run up a bill of £18, which almost ruined her father. In Keswick, Mary found letters addressed to Hatfield from his wife and the story achieved great notoriety. He was traced to Cheshire and then to Wales where he was arrested before finally being brought to trial at the assizes in Carlisle. Throughout the trial he was perfectly composed. He was found guilty and sentenced to death, not for bigamy, but for franking letters while posing as a Member of Parliament and obtaining money by forgery. Saturday, 3rd September, 1803 was the date set for his execution and the previous night the gallows were erected just outside the town. Even now Hatfield was calm, cheerful and polite to everyone at the prison. The next day the sheriffs and bailiffs arrived at the door of the jail with a post-chaise and hearse. He was pinioned before being taken to the gallows where a huge crowd had gathered. After his execution he was placed into a coffin and buried in the churchyard far away from the other tombs.

Mary of course was heartbroken, but after a little while when she had recovered slightly, she began to rather enjoy the sympathy shown to her by people all over the country. She became the heroine of ballads and plays and money was raised for her. Eventually she met a local farmer, a kind honest man, and they were happily married. When she died she was buried in the churchyard at Caldbeck. (see page 45).

Sir Gawaine and the 'Fair Lady

DURING Saxon times King Arthur often visited the city of Carlisle, accompanied by many of his knights. Here they held tournaments and jousts and the following legend is supposed to have originated. The story may well have been the basis on which Chaucer founded his "Wife of Bath's Tale." The legend concerns Sir Gawaine, one of King Arthur's knights who was with the king and Queen Guinevere in Carlisle.

Everyone had gathered from far and near to King Arthur's court, for it was Christmas and there were to be many celebrations. As they sat eating and drinking one day a girl entered and knelt before the king, begging a favour of him. She asked him to avenge her of a wicked baron who lived near Hesket on the road from Penrith. The baron lived in a castle which stood near a lake, and flags and banners flew from the castle battlements. But neither knight or lady could pass the castle wall without misfortune befalling them. The girl and her lover had been passing the castle the previous day when the baron had appeared, and after misusing her had carried off her lover. She had threatened that she would ask King Arthur for help, but the baron had merely laughed and said that the king should meet him if he dared. In a rage King Arthur vowed that the wicked baron should be punished, and immediately set off for the castle.

When the king stood before the baron, he suddenly found that all his strength had left him, and he was quickly overpowered. The baron then told him that he would only spare his life if, by the following New Year's Day, he could tell him what all women most desired. The king set off at once on his quest to find the answer to this problem, but everyone he met gave him a different answer. Some women told him wealth, others flattery, mirth, pretty clothes. As New Year's Day approached the king's agitation increased and he seemed no nearer a solution.

Then while he was out riding he saw a girl dressed in red, sitting by a green holly bush. As he approached he could see that the whole of her face was grossly mis-shapen. The maiden told the king that she would give him the answer to the problem set by the wicked baron if he would bring her a handsome knight to marry. King Arthur agreed to do this and so she told him that what all women most desire to have is their own way. The king galloped off to tell the baron, who agreed that he could go free.

King Arthur returned to Carlisle and told Queen Guinevere that, although he had answered the problem set by the wicked baron, he now had to find a husband for the ugly maiden who had given him the answer. Sir Gawaine, a loyal knight, immediately offered to marry the girl and so the wedding was arranged. On their wedding night Sir Gawaine was astonished when suddenly his ugly bride was transformed into a beautiful maiden. She explained that a cruel spell had been put on her which would be partially broken when she married a knight. Now, she could be beautiful by day or night, and he could choose which he preferred. Sir Gawaine told her that he loved her, and so she could have her own way. Now the spell was broken completely and the maiden told him that she would be beautiful always. She told Sir Gawaine that when her father was old he had married a lady who had proved to be unfaithful. The woman had put a spell on her that she would remain mis-shapen until a knight agreed to marry her. She would not be fully released from the spell until he had declared that she should always have her own way. The woman had also put a spell on her brother, turning him into the wicked baron. Now the spell had been broken, he too would be free and become once more a gentle knight.

This is only one of the many legends of King Arthur said to have occurred in the Lake Counties. There are many places which claim connections with him. His father, who was Uther Pendragon, lived in Pendragon Castle in the Mallerstang Gorge on the banks of the river Eden.

The Three Outlaws of Carlisle

A DAM BELL, Clym of the Clough and William Cloudisley were three outlaws who lived in Inglewood Forest near Carlisle. Although two of the outlaws were not married, William had a family in Carlisle and he longed to visit them. Eventually he decided he must go to them, and somehow he managed to enter the city unnoticed where he was happily re-united with his wife. Unknown to William, however, the old woman who was a lodger in the house crept away and betrayed him and soon the sheriff's men were banging at the door. Bravely, William's wife guarded the front door with an axe while William was shooting at the sheriff's men through the windows, but it was in vain. The sheriff's men set fire to the house, and William was captured as he ran from the blaze. He was marched off to prison and it was declared that he would be hanged the following day.

While William was in jail, Adam and Clym were being warned by the son of a swineherd they had previously met in the forest, and whom William had befriended. He ran back to the forest from Carlisle and told them that William was to be hanged. Immediately Adam and Clym set of in the direction of the city determined to free him. Night had fallen by the time they reached Carlisle, and in the darkness they murdered the porter, stole his keys, and waited.

The next day dawned and William was led to his execution. Adam and Clym were ready, and their plan had been well laid. At exactly the right moment two arrows were sent winging from their bows and the sheriff and the justice fell dead in the market square. Pandemonium followed during which the townsmen helped to free William and there was a fierce battle, the three outlaws killing many men. Some claimed three hundred men died that day including the Mayor of Carlisle, bailies and constables and serjeants of the law. Somehow amid the confusion the three outlaws made good their escape, leaving the city in chaos.

Once back in Inglewood Forest they decided that their only chance of pardon was to confess to the king the crimes for which they had been outlawed, before news reached him of the events of that day. They hurried to London, but when the king heard their confession he ordered that they should all be hanged. The queen however intervened on their behalf, and as a special favour the king agreed to their being given a pardon. They were only just in time, for almost immediately messengers arrived from the north with news of the murders committed in Carlisle. Of course once the king's word had been given it could not be revoked and the three outlaws were free men, though the king was very angry. He decided to test these three men from the north, who had caused so much trouble, and so he ordered his best archers to compete against them.

William refused to shoot in the butts and instead aimed at a hazel wand and split it in two. Then he brought forward his seven-year-old son and standing the child in front of a stake placed an apple on his head. He declared that he would split the apple at six score paces. The king warned him that if the child was harmed the three outlaws would surely hang. William aimed and the arrow split the apple— the child was unharmed. After this the outlaws took the king's "cloth and fee." They were paid eighteen pence a day and remained his men until they died.

St. Kentigern

THE mother of Kentigern was a royal princess, Thenew, who enraged her father the King of Cambria by her refusal to marry Ewan, a chieftain, about the year A.D. 518. The king was so incensed that he gave his daughter the choice of marrying Ewan or being sent away to spend her life as a servant-girl. Rather than break the promise she had made to lead a pure life, she chose to go away. However the chieftain waylaid her and forced her to break her vow of purity. In due time her condition became apparent and the punishment was stringent—she was condemned to death by stoning. Somehow she managed to survive so she was tied across the wheel of a chariot which was pushed over the top of a steep hill. Again she escaped death which made her captors all the more determined she should die. She was placed in an oarless coracle and in the evening she was pushed out to sea on the ebb tide. During the night a tremendous storm raged and her captors were at last convinced that the princess was dead. However, again by a miracle the princess survived and the next morning she staggered ashore on the coast of the Firth of Forth. That day Kentigern was born.

Thenew and her baby were given food and shelter by a Christian teacher called Servanus. In the years that followed, Kentigern became a great favourite with Servanus who called him Myn Ghu (My Friend), later pronounced Mungo. The other pupils of Servanus became very jealous of Kentigern and sought to remove him from favour. This they did by killing a robin redbreast, a pet of Servanus, and blaming Kentigern. Servanus was deeply upset but Kentigern restored the bird to life and all was well. The bird then became one of the symbols of St. Kentigern.

He began preaching in Scotland and at the age of 25 was ordained. When he learned of a plot to kill him by the pagan King Morken he travelled south to Carlisle, teaching and baptising, and from here to the Lake District. Many of the churches are dedicated to St. Kentigern or St. Mungo, and many have connections with his journeys. These include Mungrisdale or Mungo's Dale and Crosthwaite, where he spent much time teaching the Christian faith. Eventually he left the Lake Counties and travelled to North Wales where he established a monastery before returning to Strathclyde.

Many stories are told of the works of St. Kentigern, one of the most popular relating to another of his symbols, the fish. The legend is that a certain king gave his wife a ring, who in turn gave it to a knight. One day while out hunting with the king the party stopped to rest and as the knight slept the king stole the ring and threw it into the nearby river. When they returned the king ordered the queen to return the ring to him, stating that if the ring was not returned within three days she would be put to death. The queen, on hearing from the knight that the ring had been stolen, sought help from St. Kentigern. After prayer, he ordered that a hook should be cast into the river and the ring would be found inside the salmon which would be caught. The ring was indeed recovered and the queen's life saved. A stone carving of a fish over the doorway of the church at Kirkcambeck, which is dedicated to St. Mungo, is a reminder of this story.

All St. Kentigern's symbols, a fish, a bird, a tree and a bell, can be seen in the church at Crosthwaite (see Crosthwaite Church, page 46).

The Spectre Army of Souter Fell

SOUTER FELL which lies to the east of Skiddaw and Blencathra is the setting for a phenomenon which cannot be fully explained, though many have tried. This is the sudden appearance of a large army which has been seen clearly on numerous occasions marching across the steep and lonely fell. It has been seen by too many people to be passed off as mere fancy or the result of midsummer wine. There is also the theory that it is an optical illusion, the result of the sun's rays on certain cloud formations, but this would not explain why it was always seen on Midsummer Eve.

The spectre army was first seen in 1735 by a servant of William Lancaster of Blakehills. The servant was about half a mile from the fell when to his amazement he saw on the east side of the mountain an army marching. It appeared over some rising ground and disappeared over a precipice near the top of the fell, and its numbers were so great that he was able to watch for about an hour. However, as no-one else had seen the army the servant was ridiculed and the story ignored.

Two years later, however, again on Midsummer's Eve, William Lancaster also saw the spectre army. He saw troops five deep following five mounted soldiers, exactly where his servant had seen them previously. He called to his family and as they watched they saw one of the five mounted soldiers gallop ahead to order the march, before returning to his position at the head of the ranks. Gradually the troops became more disorganised, no longer marching in rank, but they continued to march till it was too dark for William Lancaster to see them. As with his servant, William Lancaster and his family were ridiculed for what they had claimed to have seen and again the matter was forgotten.

The spectre army was not seen again until the Midsummer Eve before the last Scottish rebellion. Again it was seen by William Lancaster and his family, but this time they were determined to have reliable witnesses present so that there could be no doubt as to the authenticity of their claim. They hurriedly assembled twenty-six reliable people who later swore before a judge that they had seen the army. According to their reports the number of troops was immense, stretching for almost half a mile and marching for over an hour, again until darkness fell. As well as the troops they saw a number of carriages, and again the troops and horses travelled over the rough and rocky fell-side before disappearing over a precipice. This time, in addition to William Lancaster and his witnesses, many of the local people living within a radius of about a mile also saw the marching troops, some claiming to have watched for almost two hours.

3: Places of Interest

Bewcastle

Route: Take the A6071 from Brampton; in approximately 1½ miles turn right on unclassified road to Walton and Nickies Hill, where join the B6318. Turn right and in one mile left. Follow signs to Bewcastle.

FAMED for its cross, this small village is steeped in history. Here we see the remains of a Roman fort where once 1,000 men were stationed, perhaps to prevent Scots raiders from reaching the wall, and within these ancient fortifications stand the castle, church and cross.

The fort, built in about A.D. 120, had a double line of ramparts, the positions of which can still be seen. Excavations over the last century have revealed the base of an altar and silver plaques, together with nine inscribed stones, one with a dedication to Cocidus, which is now in Tullie House Museum, Carlisle (see page 55). After the withdrawal of the Roman garrison the fort was appropriated by Anglo-Saxons, who erected the cross, and later by Norsemen. One of their chiefs, Beuth, built the castle—Bewcastle. After the Norman conquest the land passed to William de Meschines and during the latter part of the 12th century, in the reign of Henry II, to the de Vaux family. Built with stones from the Wall, the ruined tower and part of the walls are all that remain from their destruction in 1641, but they still show a one time greatness.

Built at the same time as the castle was the church, also with stones from the Wall. All that remains of this period is the east wall with its small lancet windows. During the early part of the 16th century services were not carried out in the church, and by 1597 it was said to have been in a ruinous state for over 60 years. Records show that the church was rebuilt in 1792 and again restored in 1901. There is an interesting old grave slab near the west wall.

The lovely Bewcastle cross was built in the latter half of the 7th century and it has brought fame to the village. This cross and the one at Ruthwell are unique examples of the craftsmanship of the period. The carvings on the four faces of the 14 foot shaft are in excellent condition, but particularly interesting are those on the west face.

Bewcastle Cross

This has four panels; at the top is St. John the Baptist carrying the Agnus Dei, and below is Christ standing on a lion and adder, a hand raised in blessing. A runic inscription follows with a falconer at the base—maybe representing St. John the Baptist. The south face contains five panels of differing scroll and knot designs and a sundial marked in twelve divisions. The east side is one complete panel of a vine scroll. The north side has again five panels, the top and bottom being of a vine scroll, the next two are knot work and the centre panel is chequer work. The cross head is missing.

Brougham Castle

Route: A66, 1½ miles east of Penrith. Opening times: Sundays at 2 p.m., closing as under. Daily, March–October 9.30–5.30; May–September 9.30–7; November–February 10–4.30. Admission: Adults 5p, Children 2½p. Season tickets allowing access to all Ministry of Buildings and Works properties—75p per annum.

DURING the time of the Roman occupation, Brougham commanded a strategic position on the banks of the river Eamont where Agricola established the fort of Brocavum. This site continued

Brougham Castle

to be of importance and, in the reign of Henry II, Brougham was granted to Gospatric, son of Orm. In 1180 the keep was built, together with ancillary buildings defended by a strong stockade and ditch. It is likely that at this time the remains of the Roman fort served as an outer bailey. Towards the end of the century the lands passed to the Vipont family who strengthened the defences by heightening the keep and adding an inner gatehouse and a south-west tower.

In 1273 the marriage of Isabel Vipont to Roger de Clifford brought this renowned family into the affairs of Brougham Castle. Many of the Cliffords made extensions and alterations to the castle. The outer gatehouse was built in 1300 by Robert who died fourteen years later at the Battle of Bannockburn; and a stone which stated "Thys made Roger" probably refers to work carried out by the Fifth Lord Clifford in 1383. This inscribed stone was lost for over three hundred years but in the 19th century it was found in the bed of the stream, and re-set in its present position above the entrance to the outer gatehouse.

The Civil War brought almost complete destruction to the castle and in 1651 Lady Anne Clifford, perhaps the best remembered of all the family, began her work. She instigated a vast programme of repair and rebuilding, not only at Brougham but also at the Clifford estates of Appleby, Brough, Pendragon and Skipton. After her death in 1676 her successors, the Earls of Thanet, neglected the estates and by 1714 Brougham was again in ruins. In the 19th century the estates passed to the Tufton family and were given to the nation in 1928. Brougham Castle is now under the care of the Department of the Environment.

The castle is entered via the outer gatehouse where a portcullis groove can still be seen. The gate hall has the inscription recording Lady Anne's many titles, and the room over the gate-house has a 17th century fireplace and window recesses which still have the old window seats in place. The second floor room, known in Lady Anne's time as the painted chamber, contains in its north wall an opening to the wall passage leading to a stairway. The oldest portion of the castle is the keep or pagan tower which is 45 feet square with walls 11 feet thick. It has a spiral stairway which once led from the vault to all the upper floors. On the second floor is a short wall passage connected with the stairway, and in its ceiling is a Roman tombstone. The wording of the inscription suggests that it commemorated the death of an early Christian. The additions made to the castle over the centuries can be traced clearly through their differing styles, and features of architectural interest are found in the great chamber, great hall, kitchens, chapel block and the Tower of League (see also page 44).

Carlisle

THE history and associations of the city date back to the Roman occupation, the building of Hadrian's Wall and the bloody wars between the English and the Scots. Today only parts of these historical remains are accessible to the public—the Castle (page 31), the Cathedral (page 45) and Tullie House museum (page 55). It is possible to walk round part of the west walls from the tithe barn in the churchyard of St. Cuthbert's church. The barn was built by Prior Goodibour in the 15th century for the storage of his tithes. The walls lead past the cathedral, but at the Deanery turn right through the cathedral gateway built in 1527. The main doors will probably be shut but access may be obtained through the small side door, open during the day-time. From the cathedral precincts turn left into Castle Street—Tullie House museum is on the left. Continuing down this road, the castle is ahead.

Carlisle Castle

Opening times: May–September 9.30–7; *October* 9.30–5.30 (*Sundays* 2–5.30). *November–February* 9.30–4 (*Sundays* 2–4). *March–April* 9.30–5.30 (*Sundays* 2–5.30). *Admission: Keep,* 7½*p. Free access to walls and outer buildings at all times.*

CARLISLE CASTLE stood on the highest point along the river Eden where it served to guard the Scottish border. The first building was erected in 1092 by William Rufus on the site of an ancient British camp or "caer," from which is derived the city's name. This Norman castle was almost certainly a palisaded wooden structure. In 1122, Henry I fortified the city with "a castle and tower," and in 1133 the king sent his confessor Aethelwulf to be the first bishop of the new see of Carlisle. After Henry's death, Stephen de Blois usurped the English throne, but David, King of Scotland, sent troops across the border in support of his niece Matilda's claim to the throne. Stephen was forced to concede and Carlisle became a Scottish city. After David's death in 1153 the castle was handed over to Henry II in 1157, at which time the keep and curtain wall were built.

A succession of attacks and sieges continued throughout the reigns of Richard I, John, Edward I and Richard II, and the resultant necessity for repairs and rebuilding was ever present. Such repairs often involved the re-use of masonry taken from the old Roman camp at Stanwix across the river, and the typical "diamond broaching" wrought by the Roman masons can be seen on many of the red sandstone blocks. Further additions and alterations took place during the 14th and 15th centuries. By the middle of the 16th century the castle was in such a state of disrepair that Henry VIII found it necessary to replan and modernise the fortifications to facilitate the growing use of artillery. Again, some few years later, Elizabeth I made further extensions and additions.

Consisting of an outer bailey and inner enclosure of almost three acres, the castle was divided from the city by two ditches and connecting walls. The open space between castle and city was known as the glacis, and the outer ditch which originally held water was spanned by a drawbridge. In the west wall of the glacis is the small square tower named Tile Tower, also known as Richard III Tower since his crest showing a white boar is carved on a stone in the south wall. At the entrance to the outer gatehouse, the slots which once held the portcullis mechanism can still be seen.

Another moat with drawbridge separated the outer bailey from the inner bailey and gave access to the inner gatehouse, known as Captain's Tower. This three-storeyed structure dates from the 14th century and has a passage with pointed tunnel vaulting. In this can be seen traces of the small openings through which the defenders could pour boiling oil upon their intruders. The inner ward contains the keep or Great Tower, first erected in the 12th century but almost entirely rebuilt in Tudor times. Within this tower were the prisoners' cells and here, wherever sufficient light fell, the prisoners have left evidence of their captivity. Their carvings, patiently scratched with a nail point, include animals, coats of arms and scenes of a religious nature which hopefully comforted them during their incarceration.

Mary Queen of Scots visited the castle in 1568. At first she and her retinue were lodged as guests in private apartments in the tower, but later she remained as the prisoner of Elizabeth. From 1644–5 the castle was in a state of siege and "siege coins" were struck in the latter year. Some of these coins, in addition to a vivid account of the siege written by Isaac Tullie, are now preserved in Tullie House Museum. A hundred years later Prince Charles entered the city. He proclaimed his father rightful King of England at Carlisle Cross and then continued his march southward. After the final defeat at Culloden Moor prisoners filled the cells at Carlisle Castle. One of these prisoners was Major Donald MacDonald, featured in Sir Walter Scott's *Waverley* as the character "Fergus McIvor."

The dungeons still retain their horror, showing the holes for iron staples which held the prisoners in chains, and the dank, dark airlessness of these stone-lined cells. The history of Carlisle Castle as a fighting base ended with the defeat of the Stuarts. Since 1702 the castle has housed the Border Regiment, and in 1932 the Regimental Museum was opened. At the time of writing this museum is being rehoused in the Queen Mary Tower, and is scheduled for re-opening in the summer of 1972.

Cockermouth Castle

Route: North of the A66 (A594) in Cockermouth. Open: When Lord Egremont is not in residence. Monday–Friday 9.30–6; Saturday 9.30–noon and 2–4; Sundays 2–4. Guided tours including dungeons and Mirk Kirk, Monday–Friday, at 11, 2 and 4; Saturday and Sundays at 3. Admission: Adults 5p, Children 2½p. Additional charge for tours, Adults 5p, Children 2½p.

THE castle stands on the hill overlooking the rivers Derwent and Cocker, by which it is protected on two sides. The first building was probably 12th century, but what we see today are the ruins of the 13th and 14th centuries. The structure is divided into two groups, with an inner and outer bailey. The rooms to the north of the inner bailey were built in 1360, those of the south range and the kitchen tower being added in 1380 over the original protective ditch. The flagtower and the outer gatehouse were built in 1400 by Henry Percy, 1st Earl of Northumberland, and the walls are seven feet thick. Above the gateway are five coats of arms symbolising the uniting of the great estates of west Cumberland from the 15th century, when William son of Duncan II, King of Scotland, married Alice de Rumeli of Skipton. These estates were administered from the castle from the late 14th century. The gatehouse is the only part of this ancient castle which is still habitable.

Buildings of the inner gatehouse include the oubliette or secret dungeons reached by trapdoors—visits to these are included in the guided tours. Here also was a drawbridge. To the north of the gatehouse stands the two-storey roofless kitchen tower. Records show that in 1477 shingles at 3s. per hundred were used to repair the roof. In 1461, during the Wars of the Roses, the castle was subdued by the Yorkists under Lord Montagu. One storey of the tower was the kitchen where two fireplaces can still be seen. Below is a room with a vaulted ceiling, known as the "Mirk Kirk" or dark chapel, reached by a spiral staircase. The chapel was founded about 1221 and is included in the tour.

By 1598, when Mary Queen of Scots visited Cockermouth, the castle was not in a fit state to entertain her. In 1648 the castle was besieged by Sir William Hudleston, as a royalist stronghold, and after three months Cromwell himself received the surrender. Accommodation in 1679 consisted of a kitchen, a dining room, four bedrooms, stables, a courthouse, bakehouse and cellars. Until the 19th century the castle was seldom visited by its owners. The new Georgian wing in the outer bailey was completed in 1805 and is now the residence of Lord Egremont. Castle muniments dating from the 15th century are available for study by arrangement with the County Archivist. (see drawing on page 42)

Lorton Hall, Cockermouth

The home of the Rev. J. A. Woodhead-Keith-Dixon
Route: 4 miles south of Cockermouth on B5289. House and Gardens are open Bank Holidays, and at other times by appointment. Admission: Adults 15p, Children 10p.

IN A.D. 850 it is said that monks carrying the body of St. Cuthbert rested at Lorton. A chapel was built which remained in use for the village until the Reformation, and later for the family. Records show that by 1578 it was in a state of great decay, and in 1630 it was converted into farm buildings, only being restored and re-consecrated in 1965. The original pele tower round which the rest of the house was built probably dates from 1050, and it would have been here that King Malcolm III and Queen Margaret of Scotland stayed when visiting their kingdom of Strathclyde in 1089. The present pele tower dates from the 15th century and is joined to the chapel block by a

Lorton Hall

medieval range of domestic quarters which were completed with a classical front in 1663. This date is inscribed above the original front door which now leads on to the Fountain Court. Charles II stayed at the Hall during a secret visit to Cumberland to rally supporters in 1653. The king was received by Mrs. Mary Winder, then Lady of the Manor, who vowed that the day the king was restored to the throne she would plant one of his favourite trees, a beech. This she did on 29th May, 1660, and the tree is still standing.

The present house remains much as it was originally. In King Charles' room on the first floor a priest's hole has been discovered which may connect with another found in the dining room. Further recent restorations have revealed a complete fireplace of 1630 in another bedroom. Oak panelling is a feature of the house which also contains some excellent examples of Jacobean and Carolean furniture. Of especial interest is a Charles II rocking chair and a fine oak court cupboard. This is a "lived in" family home which has belonged to the Winder and Dixon families in descent from the original pre-Conquest Norse owners. The Hall is said to be haunted by an 18th century member of the Winder family. She is known as "The Grey Lady" and has been seen wearing a grey gauzy dress and carrying a lighted candle.

Wordsworth House, Cockermouth (National Trust)

Route: On A66 (re-numbered A594). Open: Easter Saturday–end of September except Fridays and Sundays 10.30–12.30 and 2–4.30. Admission: Adults 10p, Children 5p.

A GEORGIAN house built in 1745 for the Sheriff of Cumberland, and later let to John Wordsworth by the Earl of Lonsdale who acquired it some years later. William was born here in 1770 and spent the first thirteen years of his childhood in the house until the death of his father in 1783, when he was sent to guardians at Hawkshead. Only two rooms of the house are shown to the public; the dining room on the left of the hall and the sitting room on the first floor. The dining room has an elaborate plaster ceiling and is furnished with pieces belonging to the family. The bureau was Wordsworth's and contains many of his books. On the table are pieces of Crown Derby china and on the display shelves is a unique collection of Rockingham and Spode tulips. The sitting room contains many interesting pieces of period furniture; on the wall hangs a painting by Turner of Killgarrin Castle in Wales. The terrace where William and Dorothy used to play is still to be seen although much of the garden has been changed. Before leaving the house notice the ceiling in the room opposite to the dining room; this room is not open to the public although the door is often left open.

Corby Castle

Route: A69 out of Carlisle; turn at Warwick Bridge. Opening times: Grounds Thursday 2–7. The house is not open to the public. Admission: 5p.

CORBY CASTLE stands on the east bank of the river Eden and is almost 90 feet above the river. The first building must certainly have been a Pele Tower and was probably erected during the 13th century by the Salkeld family. All that is now visible of this tower is part of its spiral stairway and some thicker sections of the wall which are located at the entrance side of the house. Two right hand bays represent the site of the tower. The Salkeld family owned the Manors of Great and Little Corby until 1611 when the properties were sold to Lord William Howard, third son of the Duke of Norfolk. Lord William built the house on to the back of the existing Pele Tower making the whole structure an "L" shaped building of two storeys one room deep. In 1809, Henry Howard commissioned Peter Nicholson, a well-known north country architect, and had the house transformed into a square Georgian mansion. A new east front was joined on to the Pele Tower and a new south front was also added. Only the west front has the original 17th century stonework, the rest being encased in red sandstone which was quarried in the grounds.

There has always been a Catholic chapel at Corby and the present chapel is in the house, having been moved from its external position at the time of the alterations. The rebuilding programme took eight years to complete. It is interesting to note that since the time when Lord William and Lady Howard came north to Cumberland there has always been a branch of the Howard family living at Corby Castle. After paying a prodigious fine to the crown for their family's participation in the affairs of Mary Queen of Scots, the Howards settled at Naworth Castle and bought Corby for their second son, Sir Francis.

The grounds, now the only part of the property open to the public, were landscaped by Lord William's grandson Thomas Howard who lived at Corby until 1730. They stretch along the banks of the river Eden for about a mile with trees, shaded walks, lawns, a summer house and a lodge. The Historic Buildings Council gave a grant in 1957 and some of this money was used to restore the cascade which takes the water from the park down steps to the river. A statue of Lord Nelson was placed in this basin after the Battle of Trafalgar. On the path leading down from the cascades to the river is a very large stone figure: Polyphemus, who stands almost 10 feet high, holds Pan pipes in his hand and is known locally as "Belted Will," the nickname given to Lord William Howard. Below the lawns is a stone grotto with mermen, gods and goddesses who watch over the waters as they cascade into the pool beneath. From here there is a green walk leading to the small temple where musical entertainments have some-times been held, either on the steps or the platform.

Dacre Castle

Home of Mr. and Mrs. A. Kinsman. Route: 6 miles west of Penrith between B5288 and B5320. Open by written appointment only from April to September. Admission: Adults 20p, Children 10p.

HISTORY tells us that a monastery existed in Dacre in the 7th and 10th centuries. The castle was probably built on that site early in the 14th century as a border stronghold to prevent the Scots entering England. It is a massive keep with four watch towers and walls eight feet thick. During the 16th and 17th centuries the castle was seldom inhabited, but in 1675 was restored by the Earl of Sussex. Scheduled as an ancient monument, the castle has been modernised and trans-formed by the present owners, but in many ways still retains its original appearance.

The moat has been filled in, daffodils, rowans and flowering cherries have been planted and peacocks strut in the grounds. Inside, Aubusson tapestries hang on the stone walls and furniture of the Chippendale, Sheraton and Queen Anne periods blend well with pieces from France, Italy and China. In the main hall there is an attractive 1320 trefoil-headed lavabo or water drain, and the ancient fireplaces retain the original stone arch surrounds. An interesting

Dacre Castle

feature of the King's Room or solar above, is the original stonework hung with 16th century Flemish tapestries. It is said that a treaty was signed in this room between the kings of Scotland and England. This castle, the original home of the Lords of Dacre for three centuries, looks sombre from the outside, but inside it is a place of charm and colour and has all the interest of bygone days blended with the comfort of today's world (see also the church, page 47).

Hutton-in-the-Forest, Penrith

The home of Lord Inglewood. Route: North from Penrith on B5305; turn on to unclassified road near Skelton. Open: By appointment with the head gardener, telephone Skelton 265. Gardens open all the year; house when administratively possible. Admission: House and Gardens 25p; Gardens only, 12½p.

THIS is a great mansion built between two pele towers. The northern tower, with the usual vaulted ground floor and spiral staircase, was probably built by Thomas de Hoton who died in 1362. The southern tower was almost completely rebuilt in the early 1800s. In the 17th century the house was owned by Sir Henry Fletcher who built the long gallery; further buildings were added in the 17th and 19th centuries. It contains a wealth of beautiful carving, especially on the staircase, 18th century plaster ceilings, tapestries and a fine collection of period furniture. Standing, as the name suggests, in the ancient Forest of Inglewood, the house is surrounded by magnificent trees, formal gardens and terraces and a visit is well worthwhile.

Hutton John

The home of Mr. and Mrs. J. A. Hudleston. Route: West of Penrith off the B5288. Open: By appointment—telephone Greystoke 326. Weekdays from 1st May–30th September.

THE original 14th century pele tower stands in the corner between additions made to the west and north in Tudor times. The northern arm has some interesting heart-shaped windows; above one of the upper windows can be seen a cross carved for Andrew Hudleston in 1662. The great carved staircase and fine plaster ceiling in this wing are of the same date. The gardens are delightful with extensive views and are seen at their best when the roses are out. An unusual rockery of limestone has been formed by the hard water from a nearby spring, which it is said, will turn moss into stone. Magnificent yews, over 100 years old, stand near the terraces which were constructed at the same time as the house.

Kirkoswald Castle

Route: B6413 north of Penrith. At the top of the hill turn right and immediately sharp left. Free access.

THE castle, founded in 1200 and built by Ralph Engayne, had an active life of 500 years. It is built on high ground with extensive views of the valley and the Pennine hills. The moat which surrounds the castle was added in the 15th century, and although overgrown can still be traced. A high turret is the main part of the ruin, containing a damaged spiral staircase and evidence of the vaulted dungeons. Fragments of two other towers and the gatehouse can be found in the undergrowth. After the destruction of the castle in the 17th century the fine collection of paintings of English kings, which once hung in the great hall, was sent to Naworth Castle for safe keeping, later to be destroyed by fire. Although overgrown this is an interesting ruin to explore—however, we suggest that strong shoes should be worn as a field has to be crossed first (see also the college, below, and the church, page 51).

The College, Kirkoswald

Home of Mr. T. R. Fetherstonhaugh. Route: On B6413 north of Penrith. Open: By written appointment only from the summer 1972. Admission charges were not known at the time of going to press.

IN 1523 Lord Thomas Dacre founded a college at Kirkoswald for a provost and seven priests, the accommodation that was needed being added to an existing pele tower. Evidence of this can be found in the walling adjacent to the tower. The life of the college was short about 25 years, following the edict of Thomas Cranmer and the dissolution of the monasteries.

Henry Fetherstonhaugh acquired the property in 1590 and it has remained in the family ever since, history having played its part in their lives. The unfortunate Sir Timothy, son of Henry, was executed at Chester in 1651 for his part, on the king's side, in the Civil War. Shortly after this, records show that Lady Bridgett, his widow, had a house of six rooms, two bedrooms, drawing room or parlour, gallery, kitchen and old college dairy store. Of this period the fine panelling in the oak room is dated 1639; here also is the elaborately carved Jacobean chimney piece of 1641.

Much of the building as it is seen today was added in 1696, including the main front and doorway. Inside, the hall has a stone floor and carved beams, and the lovely staircase has twisted balusters and carved stair ends. Above the fireplace stands a large sandstone carving of the Dacre coat of arms. The carving was saved from the 16th century wing of the college (demolished to make way for the 1696 building) and placed on the outside wall of the stables. In 1920 it was removed from its exposed position, where the weather was having a detrimental effect on the carving, and placed where it stands today. The college contains some excellent examples of period furniture which have been acquired over the years by various members of the family. There is also an interesting display of weapons of the 17th, 18th and 19th centuries (see the castle, page 38, and the church, page 51).

Whitehall, Mealsgate

Route: A595 Carlisle to Cockermouth road. Open: On application to Mr. W. C. Parkin-Moore, 5, Eton Villas, London, N.W.3. Admission free.

WHITEHALL was once a great manor house, built on three sides of a courtyard, the original date of which is not known. It is thought that Laurence Salkeld rebuilt the house in 1589, but by 1794 it was in a ruinous state. The pele tower built in 1399 is now all that remains. This is a rectangular tower of three storeys with an embattled parapet. To the south is a two storey extension with a large attic room, the whole being a good example of a border pele tower.

Pele towers were built throughout Cumberland and Westmorland in the 13th to 15th centuries, and were often incorporated into churches and private houses as a refuge against Scots raiders. The walls were exceptionally thick, seven feet not being unusual. The ground floor was tunnel vaulted and contained a spiral stairway leading to upper floors.

Penrith Castle

Opposite Penrith station. Free access.

THE original tower was built by William Strickland in 1397 when licence to crenellate was granted to him. Strickland's life as a churchman first brought to him the Bishopric of Carlisle and later he became Archbishop of Canterbury. The first massive square structure consisted of an outer wall and moat, and the entrance was a double gateway defended by the Red Tower. There were two storeys, the first floor kitchens and serving rooms and the ground floor which had a hall and a solar. When Ralph Nevill, Earl of Westmorland, received "the town and manor of Penrith" from Richard II, he made improvements to the castle and added a gatehouse and guardrooms. Another and later member of the Nevill family to occupy the castle was Richard, Earl of Warwick and Salisbury, known as the "King Maker."

In the mid-15th century Richard, Duke of Gloucester took up his position as Lord Warden of the Western Marches and, although he was Governor of Carlisle Castle, he lived for much of the time at Penrith. With his accession to the throne as Richard III he made major additions to this northern seat, and Penrith Castle was provided with a magnificent banqueting hall 50 feet long, 25 feet wide and 20 feet high. He also added a suite of private apartments gained by an external stairway.

After his reign the castle deteriorated and by 1547 it was almost completely in ruins. Over the years large quantities of stone were removed and used for various other projects, and later buildings were attached to the old castle walls. The land and castle next came into the possession of the Lancaster & Carlisle Railway Company, and then in 1913 was bought by Penrith Urban Council who placed it in the hands of the Commission for the Protection of Ancient Monuments. The site was then cleared of modern masonry and attached buildings in preparation for the excavation and the supporting of overhanging stonework which had to be undertaken.

Today one of the most impressive parts is the south wall which stands to a considerable height. Several small window embrasures are visible from the outside, and on the inside the positions of fireplaces are clearly seen. The east tower stands high, and of the north-east tower one wall remains plus the tunnel vaulting of its basement. South of the east tower is a narrow gateway and again south of this, below the solar, an oven has been uncovered showing the smoke-hole in the wall. The land surrounding the castle has been made into a municipal park with rose garden, bandstand, tennis courts, bowling greens and children's playground. The stone gateway at the entrance was built as a memorial to the dead of two world wars (see also the church, page 53).

Nunnery Walks, Staffield

Route: On the Kirkoswald to Armathwaite road (unclassified). A small charge is made for the walks, and visitors should pay at the house. There is a free car park.

ARMATHWAITE NUNNERY is an 18th century house built on the foundations of a Benedictine convent. The convent was built about 1080 but was eventually dissolved by King Henry VIII. Parts of the original walls can still be seen, to a height of approximately 2 ft. 6 ins.

On leaving the house and car park, pass through the gate and follow the path keeping right. The path crosses two fields before entering a wood where distant glimpses may be seen of the river below. Eventually the path emerges above the river Eden and there are steps down to a lower path. This leads back along the banks of the river and then to the point where it is joined by the Croglin Beck, a fast flowing tributary dropping some 1,500 feet in five miles as it comes down from the Pennines. The path follows a series of spectacular waterfalls, though care *must* be taken as it is very narrow and during or after wet weather the stones are very slippery. The path eventually leads to some steps which bring you back to the fields at the beginning of the walks. The route is not suitable for very young children or elderly people, and sensible shoes are essential. The walks are about two miles in length.

Workington Hall

THE first building on the site was a wooden structure with a thatched roof built towards the end of the 12th century by Patric de Culwen. Probably stone walls were added at a later date, and in 1379 Gilbert de Culwen received a licence to crenellate his hall. The pele tower of that date is the oldest remaining portion of the buildings; it has a vaulted basement and is surrounded on all sides by thick rubble walls. Such pele towers were built as protection against assault, but by the beginning of the 15th century times became more peaceful and manorial lords built outwards to gain more accommodation. Workington Hall thus gained three more vaulted cellars surmounted by one-storeyed "aula" or halls. In the 16th century further additions were a long wing to the south, a shorter kitchen wing to the north and a gatehouse. The hall during Tudor times has been described as a "red brick courtyard mansion" but successive generations of the Curwen family made such extensive renovations that in some instances all that was left of the original hall were the foundations and basements.

In 1568 Sir Henry and Lady Curwen welcomed to their home Mary Queen of Scots who was on her way to Cockermouth Castle and Carlisle. It was from Workington Hall that Mary wrote to Elizabeth I asking for help: "I entreat you to send for me as soon as possible, for I am in a pitiable condition, not only for a Queen but even for a gentlewoman, having nothing in the world but the clothes in which I escaped." This letter was dated "May 17th, Workington." It is said that the Curwen family were given a period travelling clock by Mary as a token of her gratitude for their kindness during her enforced stay at the hall.

Mr. John F. Curwen wrote a very detailed account of the interior and furnishings of Workington Hall in 1899, and there are also records and illustrations of many of the rooms as they appeared in 1912. Unfortunately, Workington Hall has changed hands many times since then and its condition grew steadily worse. The last private owner gave the hall to Workington Corporation in 1936 and now it stands virtually in ruins—a sad end to one of Cumberland's most historic houses (see page 57, Helena Thompson Museum).

Cockermouth Castle

4:   *Abbeys and Churches*

Abbey Town: Holm Cultram Abbey

Route: Near the junction of the B5307 and B5302 west of Carlisle.

EARLY in the 12th century three Cistercian houses were founded
in the Lake District—Furness Abbey in 1127, Calder Abbey 1134,
and Holm Cultram 1150. All were in remote valleys far from habi-
tation. Holm Cultram Abbey was established as the daughter house
to Melrose Abbey, the Solway area being under the rule of the Scots
until 1157. By 1192 the abbey was completed and the monks self-
supporting. Their habits made from undyed homespun fleece gave
them the name of the White Monks; their wool, of exceptional
quality, was shipped to other parts of the country. Profitable salt works
and iron mines were established as early as the mid-12th century.

The abbey suffered in the border raids of 1216 and 1319, and was
used as a resting place by Edward I for his army before raiding
Scotland. The original abbey buildings are thought to have been
bigger than Carlisle cathedral, the parish church now occupying only
part of the early nave. After the dissolution the abbey continued in
use as a parish church and a refuge from the Scots, a petition having
been presented to Cromwell, then chancellor, for the release of the
abbot from prison.

Unable to afford repair the parishioners allowed the abbey to fall
into ruins, the stones being used to build the local farms and houses.
Evidence of this can still be seen in the local buildings. In 1600 the
tower collapsed and repairs started; these were in turn hampered by a
fire in 1604 with further deterioration until 1724. The church, as it is
now seen, dates from these restorations. Walls were built up between
the 12th century piers of the aisles and the east end was brought
forward. The fine timber roof is probably original and has recently
been uncovered; notice also the old pulpit. Of exceptional interest is
the fine Norman west doorway with dog-tooth moulding. Built into
the porch, over the arch, can be seen the date 1507; the upper part
was added later as a vestry. Inside the porch are relics of the old
abbey—parts of the monuments to Robert Chambers, 1518; the
Earl of Carrick, father of Robert the Bruce, early 14th century; and

Abbot Rydekar, 1434. Carvings of Henry VII and his wife, with their coat of arms, are also to be seen. Beside the porch to the north is a carved niche of the early 16th century, and to the south are the remains of an original 12th century staircase leading to the roof. Excavations are taking place to find the positions of the other abbey buildings and the outer walls of the original church (see page 67, for details of a Festival of the Arts held in June).

Brougham: The Parish Church of Ninekirks

Route: These buildings lie in the angle of A686, A66 and A6, south-east of Penrith.

THIS small rectangular church, with the nave and chancel all one, was completely rebuilt by Lady Anne Clifford in 1660 in defiance of Oliver Cromwell, and was perhaps the only church to be completed during this period. In 1841 the porch was added and the Brougham vaults built, the excavations revealing some interesting tombs. The plaster on the east wall shows the date 1660 and the initials A.P. 16th and 18th century brasses of members of the Brougham families and grave covers of the 12th century are to be found in the church. The pews, screen and pulpit, with its sounding board, indicate the carving and workmanship of the 17th century. The font is dated 1662 and the poor box 1666.

Brougham Chapel

THE chapel was known to exist in 1220 and records show that it was restored during the life of Lady Anne, although perhaps not by her, as it was the property of the Byrd family. The chapel referred to as "under repair" in her diary may have been the one in the castle. The major work of restoration was carried out by Lord Brougham and Vaux between 1830–36. He filled the chapel with a profusion of Flemish carving which is indescribable, the masterpiece of which was the Reredos or altar piece. This is now on loan to the Victoria and Albert Museum, for five years, from July 1971 (see page 29, Brougham Castle).

The Countess Pillar

THE pillar which lies two miles to the east of the castle was erected by Lady Anne in 1656 to the memory of her mother who died in 1616. The commemorative inscription tells of the £4 annuity to be given to the poor of the parish on the 2nd April, a custom which is still observed.

Lady Anne, Countess of Pembroke

L ADY ANNE, a predominant figure in Westmorland during the
17th century, was born in Skipton Castle in 1589 to George
Clifford, 3rd Earl of Cumberland. At the age of 19 she married the
3rd Earl of Dorset and by the age of 34 when the Earl died she had
five children. After six years of widowhood Anne married the 4th
Earl of Pembroke, whom she outlived. Her full titles then included
Baroness Clifford of Westmorland; Lady of the Honour of Skipton;
by inheritance, High Sheriffess of Westmorland (from her father) and
Dowager Countess of Dorset, Pembroke and Montgomery. A legal
battle for her father's inheritance lasted 30 years during which time
she refused to obey a ruling given by James I. The Cromwellian period
saw the destruction of her castles and churches, which out of pique
she restored, including Appleby, Skipton, Brough, Brougham and
Pendragon castles and numerous churches. In 1655 she repaired
Appleby church and built her own vault, in which she was buried
after her death at Brougham Castle in 1676.

Caldbeck, Church of St. Kentigern

Route: On B5299 south-west of Carlisle.

T HE remains of St. Mungo's well, which can be reached by
following the path round the west end of the church and through
the gate to the river bridge, would suggest that there was some sort
of religious building here in the 6th century (see page 24 for the story
of St. Kentigern). All that remains of the Norman church of 1118, the
first stone church on the site, is the wall behind the choir seats and the
doorway with beak decoration. The original chancel arch, which is
over 800 years old, was removed to the porch in 1520 during restoration. On the north side of the chancel is a small leper window built in
the 13th century. The vestry was added in the 16th century, the
opening being made through the thickness of the wall. Standing by
this doorway is a medieval tomb slab of about 1250 to Thomas de
Brey. The church is also famed for its association with John Peel,
(see page 16,) whose grave can be seen near the church to the left of
the path. Also in the churchyard is the grave of Mary Robinson
whose story is on page 20.

Carlisle Cathedral

T HE cathedral stands on the site of one of Agricola's forts, although
the earliest mention of a christian building was made in 685 when
St. Cuthbert visited the town. Further evidence is to be found in the
arm of a Saxon Cross. In 1122 Henry I visited Carlisle and founded
an Augustinian Priory, which by 1133 had become the cathedral.
Building was completed by 1219. The remains of the original Norman

nave are now the Border Regiment Chapel, with its massive columns and clerestory with Norman windows and capitals. These were probably built with stones from Hadrian's wall. It will be seen that this part of the cathedral has at some time suffered a settlement, the columns being "out of true."

Between 1225–50 the cathedral was considerably extended to the east with the addition of the choir and presbytery. The lancet windows of this period are on the north side. Following a fire in 1292 restoration and rebuilding continued until 1380. It is this building which stands today, notably the fourteen sculptured capitals of the choir and the great east window. The choir also contains some beautifully carved misericords of the 15th century; the canopies to the stalls were added at this time as was the screen to St. Catherine's chapel by the south transept. In the north and south aisles the paintings on the back of the choir stalls, executed in the time of Thomas Gondibour, 1484–1507, should not be missed.

The Salkeld screen to the north of the presbytery, erected in 1541, marks the end of the priory and the new foundation by Henry VIII. Lancelot Salkeld was the last prior and the first dean of the Cathedral. Between 1600–50 the cathedral and priory buildings fell into a state of decay, and in 1644–5 much of the nave was pulled down after a siege to rebuild the city walls. Only two arches remain of the chapter house and these can be seen on approaching the west door. After the 1745 Jacobite rebellion the cathedral was used as a prison.

The fratry was the only priory building not destroyed, and stands on the south side of the cathedral. It has a 14th century underloft and houses the cathedral library; here also are many capes and vestments in ancient silk and velvet, one dating from 1460. Through the centuries history has played a major part in the life of the cathedral and can be traced in the ancient glass, beautiful carvings, memorials in stone and brass and other treasures too numerous to mention in detail.

Crosthwaite: Church of St. Kentigern

Route: On A66 west of Keswick.

ON THE spot where St. Kentigern planted his cross, in a clearing in the forest, stands the church we see today. The foundations of a "new" church built in 1181 can be found in the base of the north aisle wall and part of the south-west corner near the base of the tower. A chapel was added in 1340 and extensive alterations made in the 16th century. The re-dedication or consecration of the church at this time is marked by the unique consecration crosses. Of the nine internally, six are in the north aisle and only three in the south. St. Kentigern's is the only church to have a complete set of external crosses (reminders of the 12 apostles). In 1844 the church was further restored under the direction of Sir Gilbert Scott.

Entering the church, notice the great oak bolt—a safeguard against invaders. Immediately opposite is the blocked up north or Devil's Door. The tower, built during the 16th century, is kept locked, but access may be obtained with permission from the rector. By tradition the bells have always been rung on Sundays, and when there was a shortage of men, as in 1945, women would take over. At the time of the German surrender the names of four evacuated Roedean school girls were included in the register of bell-ringers. The chancel contains in the south-east corner an ancient piscina (the lid may be lifted). The floor at the altar is in tile mosaics and shows a bird, a bell, a fish and a tree with the words "En Youta Nina," meaning "In this conquer."

In the Mary Magdalene Chapel is the fine Radcliffe memorial of 1527; the brasses are about 24 inches long and show Sir John in armour and Alice, his wife, in a long gown and head-dress. Lady Alice is not buried here but in Salisbury Cathedral. Most notable among the other memorials is that in white marble to Robert Southey who preceded William Wordsworth as poet Laureate, and died in 1843— his epitaph was composed by Wordsworth. Among the other ancient curiosities in the church are the lovely 14th century font; the 15th century effigies at the south-east corner; the ancient pillow stone and the stained glass dating from the 15th century. A relic of the 12th century church is a detached cross shaft with capital, dated about 1173.

Outside notice the sundial dated 1602, high on the south wall; there is also a mass clock on the tower buttress. The tomb of Southey has recently been restored by the Brazilian Government, for whom he wrote the *History of Brazil*. A slate plinth in the churchyard indicates the position of the surrounding mountains.

Dacre: Church of St. Andrew

Route: On unclassified road between the B5288 and B5320 west of Penrith.

EVIDENCE that St. Andrew's church stands on the site of a Saxon monastery is borne out by the presence of a drain on the south side of the church. The chancel and nave are Norman, having on the north side rounded pillars; those on the south are octagonal of the 14th century. On the window sill in the chancel is a piece of cross shaft with carving showing a winged animal, probably dating from A.D. 800. Below, a larger piece of cross shaft has carving depicting the peace of Dacre in 926, when Athelstan of England, Constantine III of Scotland and Eugenius of Cumberland are said to have met on the site of the present castle.

The rather mutilated cross-legged effigy also in the chancel may be of Ranulf, 1st Lord Dacre of the 4th century. The south door is interesting—the lock and key, bearing initials and the date 1671, were given by Lady Anne Clifford, countess of Pembroke, benifactress of many churches in the area. The tiny 13th century lancet windows and the square headed priest's door in the chancel are worthy of note. The Norman tower with its original arch was rebuilt in 1810, and now has a pleasing modern door to the nave. In the churchyard and the church there are many memorials to the Hassell family. Strangely, in the churchyard are four stone bears, two of which are near the gate. No one knows why they are there; they were probably taken from the castle many years ago. (See also the castle, p. 36.)

Great Salkeld: Church of St. Cuthbert

Route: On B6421 road to Lazonby, north-east of Penrith.

FORTY churches in the north of England mark the spot where, legend tells us, monks carrying the body of St. Cuthbert rested during their flight from the Danes. The foundation of this church therefore dates to 880; building of the Norman church began about 1080 with the beautiful south doorway. In three recessed orders the carvings show an excellent example of the work of the period and include beak-head, zig-zag and emblems of Scandinavian Mythology —preserved by the building of a porch. The Norman windows in the nave were restored in 1866. The small doorway at the west end, cut through the thickness of the wall, leads to the tower built in 1380 as a fortification against the Scots raiders. Over the windows on the

Great Salkeld Church

south side of the tower, in what is now used as the vestry, are ancient grave slabs with carvings depicting a blacksmith and a knight. The carved oak vestry cupboard is dated 1681. Access to the narrow spiral staircase is through the small door in the south-east corner; permission to enter must be obtained from the rector or one of the church wardens, and children are not allowed unless accompanied by an adult. The first floor is now the ringing chamber and in the north wall is a fireplace used during the border raids. The lintel is an ancient grave cover dated 1290, the carvings showing that it belonged to a forester. The basement or cellar of the tower is tunnel vaulted, and is now used as a boiler room.

Above the vestry door hangs a Cromwellian suit of armour collected after a skirmish between the Royalists and the Scottish army in 1644. To the right of the altar lies a stone effigy of a rector of St. Cuthbert's, Thomas de Caldbeck, dated 1320. There are many other tablets and tombs both in and outside the church dating from the 14th century, the list of rectors serving the parish began in 1199. In the porch, which was built in 1750, are the remains of a small Roman altar, part of an Anglican cross-carved grave cover, and also a small font. There is a legend which says that Dick Whittington, Lord Mayor of London, was so taken with the church that he sent a peal of bells to be hung in the tower, but they never reached their destination.

Greystoke: Church of St. Andrew

Route: The church lies to the east of the A594 Penrith to Keswick road·

THE exact date of the foundation of St. Andrews is not known, although mention is made in 1255 and records tell that it was in a bad state of repair in 1382. At this time the rectory became a collegiate college, only to be dissolved by Henry VIII in the 16th century. In 1958 the college was again opened to theological students. St. Andrews is a large and spacious church, in many ways similar to Lanercost Priory. It once had six chapels and the drains of their piscinas can be seen externally in the north and south aisle. Inside near the organ are the remains of one of these.

That the graceful 13th century arch may once have supported a central tower is shown by the thickness of the wall above the arch, and its slight tilt southwards. The great east window contains in the central section 15th century glass depicting the life of St. Andrew; the glass in the lower lights is made up of fragments from a much earlier period. The upper lights and tracery are modern, showing the arms of the Howard, Dacre and Askew families, and blend well with the earlier glass. The chancel screen and the 20 canon stalls in the choir with their interesting misericords also date from the 15th century. In the south aisle is a medieval domestic table; at the west end are the recumbent figures in alabaster of the Barons of Greystoke, from 1652, and one of a British Soldier buried in Germany during the war.

On leaving the church, notice on the right in the lane the Sanctuary Stone protected by an iron grille—this marks the spot where fugitives could claim protection from the church, and beyond which they could not be arrested.

Isel: Church of St. Michael

Route: On unclassified road following the river Derwent from Cocker-mouth to Bassenthwaite Lake, north of A66 from Keswick.

THIS small Norman church has many interesting and ancient associations. The narrow south doorway is decorated with zig-zag mouldings and sheltered with a 15th century porch—notice the ancient grave slab built into the west wall. The chancel arch and the narrow, round-headed, almost Saxon style windows in the north wall all date from 1130. Behind the curtain in the south wall of the chancel is the tiny square headed priest's doorway, probably of the same period.

By the pulpit is part of a spiral staircase going nowhere—its purpose is a mystery. Over the chancel arch are the royal arms of George I, 1721. On the south window sill in the chancel is the unique Triskele Stone with rare three-armed carving; the date of this stone is uncertain —it could be as early as the 5th century but not later than the 10th. Two other fragments of 10th century cross shafts are to be found in the church. The roof contains many of the original timbers; the altar

St. Michael's Church, Isel

rails were given in 1711 but the remainder of the woodwork is of the 19th century. There are many interesting monuments both in the church and in the churchyard, mainly of the Lawson and Leigh families. In the will of Sir William Leigh, 1354, was the request that his "best horse" should be buried with him. On leaving the church notice the medieval dials cut beside the chancel window.

Across the meadows and the river Derwent stands Isel Hall, commanding extensive views of the valley. The great embattled pele tower, built to repel the border raiders, had a west wing added in the 16th century. It now presents an impressive stone facade with rows of mullioned windows. Isel Hall, ever since it was built, has been in the possession of the Leighs and their descendants. The Hall is not open to the public.

Kirkoswald: Church of St. Aidan

Route: On B6413 Lazonby to Brampton road north of Penrith. Entrance to the church is opposite the College, on the hill.

APPROACHED by a flagstone path built for the monks who lived in the college, this small church is of ancient foundation. In the 7th century, St. Aidan consecrated a church here built over the well which was once the site of Saxon "Well worshipers." The spring feeding the well, now outside the west wall, rises in the hill above the church and runs beneath the nave. The first stone church was built in 1130, of which only the base of the chancel arch remains. Further building took place in 1160–80. The nave was enlarged and the chapels added in 1240; traces of the foundations of these can be seen outside the walls. In the porch is a small stone chalice found in the grave of a priest, and here also is the arm of an old church cross. Outside the north wall are several medieval grave covers, and in the south wall a blocked up Norman doorway.

Many reasons have been given for the position of the detached tower which stands on the top of the hill behind the church. The most probable is that as the church is in a valley to the south-west, and much of the village and the castle is over the hill to the north-east, the tower was positioned in order that the bells could be heard in both directions (see also the castle, and the college, page 38.)

Lanercost Priory

Route: On unclassified road off A69 north-east of Brampton. Admission: Daily from 9.30 and Sundays from 2. Closing March–April and October at 5.30; May–September at 7; November–February at 4. Adults, 5p, Children 2½p.

FOUNDED in 1166 by Robert de Vaux and richly endowed as an Augustinian house, the priory was dedicated to St. Mary Magdalene. By 1200 the monastic buildings were complete, together with the eastern part of the church which was finished by 1220. The priory, situated so near to the Scottish border, was often used as a place of refuge by both Scots and English, and suffered pillaging and burning from both sides. Edward I stayed at the priory three times, the last being in 1306. During the dissolution of the monasteries by Henry VIII in 1536 the priory was ransacked and the monks sentenced to death after taking part in the Pilgrimage of Grace. Granted to Sir Thomas Dacre in 1559, some of the buildings were converted into a private dwelling house. It was at this time that the north aisle of the church was shut off and used as the parish church, as it is today. The remainder of the buildings fell into ruins and supplied many of the local people with the materials for their houses.

The oldest parts of the church are probably 13th century; the tall lancet windows contain fragments of 16th century glass and these, with the lovely vaulted clerestory, are the main features. In the north aisle is a cross shaft fragment with Roman lettering and carvings, the base of which is in the grass to the north of the church. The fine west front with its rich carving has, in a niche above the main door, a 13th century effigy of St. Mary Magdelene. The curtains at the west end tell the heraldic history of 800 years of the priory. In the 12th century knights wore heraldic symbols embroidered on cloth and worn over their armour—coats of arms—to identify themselves; eighteen of these arms are appliqued with felt on the curtains.

Much of the original grandeur of the abbey can be seen in the monastic ruins—the great height of the transept tower and the choir walls. The fine vaulted underloft or cellarium over 100 feet long, contains finds from the Wall and inscribed Roman altars, some of which are excellently preserved. Among the ruins can be found many ancient and interesting tombs. The prior's house which was converted into the Dacre dwelling was the last part of the priory to be occupied.

Over Denton Church

Route: On unclassified road between A69 and B6318, west of Greenhead.

THERE is no known dedication for Over Denton church, but it is thought that the first wooden church was built here in the 8th century and was the church for a Saxon settlement in the area. The later church was probably built with stones from the deserted Roman camp of Amboglana across the river Irthing to the north in 887. It is one of the earliest churches in the country. The chancel measures 12 feet by 11 feet and has an original Roman chancel arch, simple and without moulding. There are known to be only two of these arches in existence.

The nave, no bigger than a good sized living room, has a Saxon doorway in the south wall, with a square head resting on two wrought corbels. The smaller north or Devil's Door has been blocked up. These small doorways are often found in ancient churches, the superstition being that the Devil entered through the dark north door, past the font at which the child was being baptised, and out to the south in light and happiness. A small original Saxon window remains on the north of the nave—a round-headed slit with a wooden lintel. Also in the nave is an ancient coffin lid, crudely engraved with a sword and dagger. The base of the font is original although the bowl is of a later date (the original bowl is in a local garden). On the south side of the chancel is a large square opening used as a piscina. Higher up on the north side of the arch is another opening which probably contained a small charcoal fire.

The church was under the jurisdiction of the prior of Lanercost from 1169 to 1562 and a deed of 1170 referred to it as "the church of Ancient Denton." Elizabeth I granted the patronage to the Dacre family in 1562 and in 1632 this was conveyed to the Naworth family, to whom it still belongs. To the east of the church is the barn, now in ruins, which was once an ancient pele tower and was known as "The Vicarage."

Penrith: Church of St. Andrews

IT IS possible that there was a church in Penrith 1,500 years ago; it was known to be well established by 1133, with a house of Augustinian friars. All that now remains of the Norman building is the tower with walls six feet thick. On the north-west corner are the arms of the Earl of Warwick, a bear with a staff, probably of the 14th century. The nave was re-built in 1722 after it had fallen into decay following a fire. A three-sided gallery has two flights of steps and outside the entrance are the bowls of two fonts, one bearing the inscription 1661. On the wall is a plaque in memory of those who died in the plague of 1597. At the top of the steps are two stone effigies of Anthony Hutton and his wife, carved in 1637. The two brass chandeliers in the church were given by the Duke of Portland as a thanksgiving to the people of Penrith after the '45 Jacobite rising. In the vestry are three interesting medieval coffin lids. The registers date back to 1556 and are unbroken to the present day.

The Giant's Grave

IN THE churchyard are the stones marking the Giant's grave— supposedly that of Owain, King of Cumbria about 920–37. The stones are two ancient cross shafts and four hog-back stones, grouped together probably since Norman times. There is a legend that during the re-building of the church in 1722 the church wardens started to have the stones broken up, but protest from the public was so great the stones had to be repaired. Some of the rivets can still be seen.

The Giant's Thumb

THIS is a single stone probably erected by King Owain as a monument to some person of his time. Originally the shaft was surmounted by a wheel-head cross (see also the castle, page 40).

Wetheral: Church of the Holy Trinity

Route: On B6253 south-east of Carlisle.

OVER the centuries churches on this site had been burnt, pillaged and destroyed by marauding Scots until 1144 when records show that one had been established, although nothing now remains. Until the dissolution the church would have been cared for by the monks from the priory. The south window of the chancel commemorates Richard Wedderhall, prior until 1530; the oldest glass in the church is in the west window of the tower and dates from the 15th century. Even older are the 13th century round piers in the chancel.

The present church was restored in 1760 when the tower was built. In 1791 the Howard chapel was added and it is here we see the beautiful white marble memorial by Nollekens to Lady Maria Howard who died at the age of 22, after giving birth to a stillborn daughter in 1789. A niche at the east end of the north aisle contains the eroded alabaster figures of Sir Richard Salkeld and his wife Jane. He wears armour, a dagger and a sword; Lady Jane is in a long dress; and the date is 1503.

The churchyard contains some ancient tombstones — near the wall of the Howard chapel is one to Colonel Howard who died in 1643. The sundial is dated 1751 and the ancient oak tree near the church door is believed to be 1,000 years old. All that remains of the priory, founded by Ranulf Meschine in 1100 for a prior and twelve monks of the Benedictine order, is the ruined gatehouse. This was built in the 15th century and still stands to full height, with vaulted archway and windows on two storeys. The tower, now part of a farm, can be clearly seen from the churchyard. In the middle ages the priory was a sanctuary where those escaping from the law could take shelter; this included poachers from Inglewood forest who often took refuge there after being chased by gamekeepers with dogs.

Wetheral Cells or Caves are known to be of great age. There are three cut deep into the rock, above the river Eden, each measuring 20 feet by 10 feet and 9 feet high. Each chamber is lit by a rough hewn window and has a chimney in the centre. A flight of steps has been cut into the rock from the path. The caves can be clearly seen from the Corby side of the river.

5: Museums

Tullie House Museum

Castle Street, Carlisle. Open: Daily at 9. Closed April–September at
8, Saturdays at 7. October–March, closed at 5. Sundays, June–August,
open 2 30–5

BUILT in the 16th century over previous Roman buildings, the
foundations of which can be seen in the grounds, Tullie House was
for many years a private residence. Many additions have taken place
and the museum now contains a comprehensive display of antiquities
and natural history exhibits. In the entrance hall is a full size replica
of the 14 foot Bewcastle cross (see p. 27, 28), and display cases show
objects from the hoard found during tumulus excavations at Brampton in 1964. One of the most outstanding finds in Great Britain, it
includes hub fittings, chisel, fragments of scythe blade and other
implements. A room leading off the hall contains relics from the
Roman occupation of the area, including sculptures from tombs and
shrines, millstones, pottery, coins, jewelry and domestic implements.
Relief maps, photographs and details of the finds are also on display.
   The natural history section, one of the finest in the North, contains
beautifully preserved specimens of mammals, birds and fish, from
the tiny wren to the enormous tunny fish. It includes cases containing
a fox with young and a black grouse it had killed; an eagle with a
lamb; and a family of mute swans. Smaller cases show shells found
on the coast, frogs, snakes, reptiles, flies, insects and spiders. There
are large cases of land birds including kestrels, falcons and kites, and
cases of sea birds, and smaller displays showing the anatomy of
animals and how they work.
   On the first floor are the craft and guilds of the Corporation room,
which displays regalia and mementoes through the centuries. Beyond
is the section of interest to small girls, with its dolls houses, dolls and
toys. Nearby are dresses, fans and jewelry of the 18th and 19th
centuries, and cottage industries are also shown. There is a large
room of geology and pre-history showing two large murals of the
Lake District during the Ice Age and the Keswick stone circle (see
page 9). There are axe heads from the Great Langdale axe factory,

hammers and other implements, and here also is the famous Roman cauldron found at Bewcastle. An art exhibition is staged in the well lit galleries on the upper floor.

Fitz Park Trust Art Gallery and Museum

Station Road, Keswick. Route: A591–594 into Keswick from Penrith and Windermere; cross the railway and turn right over the river bridge. Open: Good Friday–end of October. Weekdays 10–noon, 2–5. Closing at 7, July and August. The museum is open in the winter by appointment for parties of not less than 10. Admission: Adults 5p, Children 2½p. School parties 1p per child.

THE museum was first opened by Peter Crofthwaite in 1781, and now houses an amazing collection of relics and antiquities, all under one roof. A remarkable model of Lakeland made by Joseph Flintoft in 1834 measures 12 feet by 9 feet and is to scale both horizontally and vertically. It is still used by walkers to plan routes through the lakes. The literary section of the museum contains many of the original manuscripts in longhand of Walpole and Wordsworth, first editions of Southey and manuscripts of Thomas de Quincey, Dr. Dalton and Ruskin. There are early photographs of the poets and a bust by Epstein. The art collection includes watercolours by Nash, Turner and Lucy Gipps. One of the most interesting recent additions is an oil painting dated 1870 by the Skiddaw Hermit, who lived in a moss hut on Dodd Fell.

Cases along one wall display 250 lakeland birds; there are also large collections of butterflies and birds' eggs.The geological section includes maps and specimens of lakeland minerals (samples may be purchased). Probably one of the largest collections of stone axes from the Great Langdale stone axe factory is displayed here, together with fragments of Roman pottery and Celtic relics including bracelets. On a Jacobean oak chest is a warning to "lift the lid carefully." Inside is a mummified cat 500 years old, found in the rafters of Clifton church, near Penrith.

One of the most remarkable exhibits is the original instrument of the Rock, Bell and Steel band, consisting of about 60 stones, 60 steel bars and 40 bells. The longest stone is about 3 feet long—the others diminish in size. They are all mounted on a frame and are hit by hammers. Invented by a mason it took three men 13 years to build. In 1848 the original band appeared by Royal Command at Buckingham Palace.

The Pencil Museum, Keswick

Route: West of the A591 to the north of the town.

THIS is a museum with a difference, where the beginnings of a pencil and its development can be seen, from the early type of manufacture in 1558 to the more scientific and modern methods of the present day. The area round Keswick has contained some of the best examples of graphite or plumbago in the world and, although this is now rare, some examples are on show. The manufacture of coloured pencils is also included. An exhibition of fine art work, executed with pencil, is on display.

Model Railway Exhibition

The Railway Station, Keswick. Route: A591–594 into Keswick from Windermere and Penrith; cross the railway and turn right over the river bridge for the station. Open: Daily except Sundays 10–9 from Easter to mid-October. Admission: 10p, children accompanied by an adult 5p.

FULLY computerised, this model railway is the most modern in the world. During the day trains travel over 100 miles, no less than 12 running at one time, their routes and performance selected at random by this revolutionary system. Between 800 and 1,000 feet of track run through model villages, countryside, tunnels, viaducts, stations and marshalling yards. Not only model railway enthusiasts but those interested in electronics will find much in this exhibition. Circuits and kits are on sale from about £5, and do-it-yourself buildings are also available. Lectures and demonstrations can be arranged if required.

Helena Thompson Museum

Park End Road, Workington. Route: Off the A595–596 coast road. Open: Tuesdays–Saturdays 10–noon and 2–4. Admission: Free.

PARK END HOUSE and its contents were given to the town of Workington by Miss Thompson, and the Georgian house was opened as a museum in December 1949. The exhibition is mainly of Victorian objects and includes costumes and costume accessories. The rooms are arranged in period and include fine furniture together with displays of silver, ceramics and glass. There is also a section of local sporting trophies. The walls are hung with pictures and prints of Old Workington, and a model of Workington Hall (see page 41) is on display.

Glasson Moss

On the Cadurnock peninsula, north of Kirkbride.

THIS nature reserve, which comes under the authority of the National Environmental Research Council, is a small portion of a formerly extensive raised bog that once extended across the peninsula. The moss itself possesses the largest area of undamaged sphagnum bog in the district, while toward the margins of the moss the land has been reclaimed and is passing into rough pasture, rush and purple moss grass. In the drier regions, birch trees are beginning to take hold, and to the north, where the ground rises fairly steeply away from the peat, swamp and birch and willow thickets have developed. One species of rare moss is found in relative abundance, and the long leafed sundew has also been found here. The public has unrestricted access.

Rockcliffe Marsh

Route: A7 north from Carlisle, over Eden Bridge. Follow signs for Rockcliffe, then for Rockcliffe Cross and Boathouse. Cars can be parked at the end of the road.

THE RESERVE stands at the confluence of the rivers Esk and Eden at the head of the Solway Firth. It covers approximately 2,000 acres of salt marsh with sand flats in the river channels. The stages of growth of a salt marsh can be clearly seen, and the development from bare sand to mature salting shows in the zones of vegetation which change according to the degree of inundation by the sea. Although the marsh is primarily a bird reserve there are areas where turf-cutting and gravel-digging take place, and there is also a valuable mushroom crop taken from the land. The bird population includes over 70 species, with greylag, barnacle and pink-footed goose, wigeon, goldeneye, mergansers, cormorant and a variety of wading birds. There is a large breeding colony of lesser black-backed gulls, and other breeding species include black-headed, greater black-backed and herring gulls, tern, redshank, oyster-catcher, lapwing, dunlin and skylark. Also to be seen are ringed plover, snipe, meadow pipit, moorhen and sheld duck.

Visitors are advised that in certain weather conditions the whole marsh may become flooded and in poor visibility route finding may be difficult. At such times it is inadvisable to go on to the marsh. The Reserve is open from February to August and access is by daily permit, free of charge, obtainable from Mr. R. Stokoe, 4, Fern Bank, Cockermouth.

Moor House

THIS extensive area of North Pennine mountain country includes Dunfell on the western escarpment and stretches eastward to the Teesdale area. The reserve covers 9,956 acres of boggy heather moorland with peat areas reaching a depth of 10 feet in some places. The district was once a grouse moor and the old shooting lodge has now been converted into a field station with laboratory facilities and accommodation for visiting scientists. The field station is under the authority of the National Environmental Research Council (formerly the Nature Conservancy). It is an excellent location for the study of geology and moorland biology and is particularly suited to experimental work. There is a public right of way across the moor, but a permit is required if one wishes to visit regions away from the right of way.

Cumberland Currant Cake

THIS is two layers of rich pastry filled with sugar and currants, and flavoured with rum. Some Cumberland folk add a little cream to the mixture. Elderberry Cake is made in a similar manner and baked in the oven. When the pie is cold it is sprinkled with a thin layer of white icing sugar, or iced.

Cumberland Ham

DIFFERENT methods of curing hams are traditional in various parts of the country. In Cumberland the hams are desalted and brown sugar added. Mutton ham is popular in this county.

Cumberland Herb Pudding

ANOTHER name for this is Easter-Ledge Pudding—it was often made at Easter from left-overs. Potatoes, vegetables and meat are mixed with leaves of Easter nettles; onion is added and boiling water poured over. The mixture is allowed to stand overnight, and then barley and oats are added, with egg, vinegar, salt and pepper. This is then put in a bag and boiled. It is eaten hot or cold, as a vegetable.

Cumberland Porter Cake

AN OLD Cumberland recipe for a very substantial cake. Butter is rubbed into flour; currants, raisins, citron, spice, lemon rind and brown sugar are added, and then a small teaspoonful of bicarbonate of soda is mixed into a bottle of warmed porter. This is beaten into the mixture and the cake baked very slowly.

Cumberland Pudding

THIS is a mixture of breadcrumbs, beef, suet, sugar, grated apples, lemon rind and treacle bound together with egg and milk and steamed for two hours. The traditional rum sauce is served with it.

Cumberland Rum Butter

A POPULAR delicacy which consists of Demerara sugar and butter beaten together, rum, nutmeg and cinnamon added to taste. In Cumberland it is spread on cream crackers or oatbread. At Christmas time it is often served with Christmas pudding. An old tradition in the Lake District was to offer wine, bread and rum butter to anyone visiting a new baby.

Cumberland Sausage

THIS sausage is sold in one long strip, not in links, and is made from pork and herbs. It is usually more expensive than ordinary sausage. Traditionally a sauce made from Bramley apples, brown sugar and a pinch of mace is served with the sausage.

Cumberland Sauce

THE sauce is served with the hams cured in Cumberland and can be used either hot or cold. The juice and rind of two oranges and one lemon are simmered; than four tablespoonsful of redcurrant jelly are stirred into the mixture until dissolved. Port wine or elderberry wine is added to taste.

Cumberland Shipped Herrings

AN OLD Cumberland recipe which makes a nourishing and tasty dish. Herrings are prepared by removing head, backbones, tails and fins. The roes are poached in salted water, then chopped and mixed with breadcrumbs and anchovy essence, chopped onion, melted butter, salt and pepper. The herrings are stuffed with this mixture, dotted with butter and baked in a fireproof dish. They are served with mustard sauce.

Cumberland Toffee

THIS toffee is very popular. It is easily made from a cup of sugar, $\frac{1}{4}$ cup golden syrup, $\frac{1}{3}$ cup of water and $\frac{1}{2}$ tablespoon butter. A pinch of salt is added. These ingredients must be melted slowly in a strong pan and then boiled until a little of the toffee forms a small ball and is brittle when dropped in cold water. Poured into a shallow greased tin, it must be marked into pieces while setting.

Solway Salmon

FINE salmon are caught in the Solway, and in the estuaries of the rivers Leven and Kent. Poached Solway Salmon is a favourite dish. The fish is put into a pan or fish kettle and covered with boiling water to which a pinch of salt and a little vinegar or lemon juice are added. Simmer the salmon for 10 minutes per pound, drain and serve with sliced cucumber and shrimp sauce, or cucumber sauce.

"Tattie Pots" or Tattie Pie

A TRADITIONAL hot pot said to be John Peel's favourite dish. It is made with potatoes, onions and Herdwick mutton. When John Peel's centenary was celebrated in October 1954 it was reported that one thousand people had "tatie pie" for dinner in the village of Caldbeck. A prize was awarded to the best singer of "D'ye ken John Peel?"

Angling

THE LAKE COUNTIES are considered by many to be one of the finest fishing areas in the country. Although some of the fishing is free, rod licences *must* be obtained from either the Cumberland River Authority for lakes and rivers flowing out to sea by way of the Cumberland coast, or from the Lancashire River Authority for those flowing by way of the Lancashire and Westmorland coasts. These licences can easily be purchased locally from a number of small post offices, hotels, or shops selling fishing tackle. On Bassenthwaite Lake a permit is also required which can be obtained from the Castle Fisheries, Cockermouth. On the main fishing rivers day, week or season tickets may be purchased from the local controlling angling association. These rivers include the Eden, Derwent, Border Esk and Ellen. Permits are required from the National Trust for fishing on Buttermere, Crummock Water and Loweswater. Fishing for salmon, brown trout, sea trout, pike, perch and rudd is popular, and there is good sea fishing in the Irish Sea and on the Solway Firth. Facilities for deep sea fishing are available at Maryport and Workington. Further details may be obtained by writing to the Cumberland River Authority, 256, London Road, Carlisle; or the Lancashire River Authority, Halton-on-Lune, Lancaster.

Fell Racing

FELL RACES, or guide races, have been a popular local sport in the Lake Counties for more than a hundred years. The race, to the top of the nearest fell and back, demands tremendous physical fitness and stamina. Most fell runners wear running boots with short spikes to help them on the steep descent. The fell race is the highlight of many of the dales sports, and to win at Grasmere Sports is the greatest achievement of all.

Fell Running

FELL RUNNING is a sport which attracts competitors from athletic and orienteering clubs throughout the north. The main events are organised by the Cumberland Fell Runners' Association and the Mountain Trial Association. The courses vary in length up to twenty miles and sometimes include as many as nine fells. Prizes are usually awarded for both individual runners and teams, and at some meetings there are prizes for winning veteran runners. For those interested in fell running further details may be obtained by writing to F. Travis, Esq., 13, Hallsenna Road, Seascale.

Fell Walking

THE scope for fell walking within the Lake Counties is boundless, but however easy the walk appears the following points should always be remembered. Weather conditions in the Lake District can change very quickly so it is important to go equipped with suitable footwear, walking or climbing boots, *not* shoes or rubber boots. Wear brightly coloured clothing, waterproof and windproof anorak and slacks or trousers. Always have a good map, compass, torch, whistle, watch and first aid kit. Do not go alone—a party of three is considered the minimum. Take careful note of weather forecasts and check on local weather conditions. *Always* before you go leave details with your friends, landlord or the police about your expected time of return and intended route, and inform them when you are safely off the fells.

Fox Hunting

FOX HUNTING is widely spread throughout the Lake Counties, both as a popular sport and also as a way of keeping down the number of foxes which threaten the livelihood of the Lakeland farmer. The mountain packs include the Blencathra, closely associated with John Peel (Keswick district); the Cumberland and Cumberland Farmers packs (John Peel country, Aspatria, Wigton and Dalston); the Melbreak (Buttermere and Loweswater); and the Ullswater (Ullswater and the Mardale fells). Most of the packs are followed on foot, and in a few instances spectators can follow by car, though care must be taken not to block the narrow mountain roads. A pair of binoculars might prove helpful for following the progress of the hounds. Meets are held two or three times a week from October to April and notices giving further details can be found locally.

Hound Trailing

IN THE past the dales farmer usually kept a small number of foxhounds which, when the hunting season was over, were raced over improvised courses. At the end of the last century the Cumberland miners took up this idea with great enthusiasm and so began the northern sport of hound trailing. Over the years the hounds have been specially bred and trained for the sport and are now much lighter and faster than the original foxhounds. The hounds follow a trail laid down beforehand by men dragging socks filled with a

mixture containing aniseed along the ground. When the trail is laid
the hounds are loosed and follow the course over the fells. The sport
is extremely popular and almost all the local agricultural shows
include a hound trail. Trails are also held on most week-days and
Saturdays during the season which lasts from Easter to late autumn.
Details can be found in local papers, and posters are usually displayed
in village shops and post offices.

Mountaineering

MOUNTAINEERING is a specialised hobby and therefore
requires a good deal of training. The Lake District Planning
Board hold week-end courses which are based on the safety aspect of
mountaineering techniques. The courses are held between September
and June at various youth hostels throughout the National Park and
include four types of instruction:

Grade I   Introductory fell walks. Use of map and compass.
Grade II   Fell navigation, mountain craft, techniques.
Grade III   Leadership, avoidance of accidents, rescue procedure.
Grade IV   Final theoretical and practical instruction.

A certificate is given on completion of the four grades which serves
as an introduction to mountaineering and rambling clubs. The fee
for the course ranges from £1.25 to £1.35. Further details may be
obtained from the Lake District National Park Planning Board,
County Hall, Kendal.

Mountaineering clubs in northern Lakeland are based at Carlisle,
Cockermouth and Keswick. Climbing meets are held in many areas
of Britain where rock, ice or snow routes are attempted.

Orienteering

ORIENTEERING is a rapidly growing sport in the Lake Counties,
where a number of events are organised each year. Members of
local clubs also travel to other parts of the country to participate in
events, journeying as far afield as Scotland and Wales. The sport
comprises a navigation test using map and compass which demands
both mental and physical ability. Events are held in areas of woodland where navigation and visibility are more difficult. The venues are
changed for each event as the sport cannot be held over familiar
terrain, and secrecy as to the exact location is vital. Final details are
not forwarded to competitors until a few days before the event. Clubs
within the Lake Counties include the Lakeland Orienteering Club,
the Border Liners Orienteering Club and the West Cumberland
Orienteering Club. Further details may be obtained by writing to
The British Orienteering Federation, 3, Glenfinlas Street, Edinburgh,
EH3 6YY.

Pony Trekking

FOR those interested in pony trekking and riding holidays the
following stables are either registered or conditionally registered

under the Riding Establishments Act, 1964. In all cases suitable clothing must be worn and some previous riding experience is preferred at most centres. Weight and height should be stated when booking.

Bassenthwaite: Mr. Archer, Robin Hood Riding and Trekking Centre, Bassenthwaite, Keswick, telephone Bassenthwaite Lake 296. Tuition and trekking available throughout the year, and accommodation if required. Unaccompanied children welcome.

Penrith: Miss D. L. Hardy, Beacon Riding School, Andrew House, Stainton, Penrith, telephone Penrith 2510. Trekking Easter and July to mid-September. Day treks. All rides accompanied.

Silloth: Mr. T. M. Brown, Silloth Riding School, Solway Holiday Camp, West Silloth, telephone Silloth 314. Hourly or afternoon treks. Rides accompanied and instruction given if required. Advance booking advisable.

Sailing

IN ADDITION to the large number of sailing craft which may be hired out by the hour or day on many of the Lakes, there are also a number of local sailing clubs. Many of these clubs offer facilities for visitors to launch sailing dinghies from their sites on payment of a small fee. Among these is the Bassenthwaite Sailing Club, situated at the northern end of the lake. Racing takes place on Thursday evenings and Saturdays and Sundays at 3 p.m. from April to October. The main class adopted for racing is the G.P.14. The climax of the season is the Bassenthwaite Sailing Week. The Derwentwater Sailing Club, situated at Portinscale, hold mixed class handicap racing on alternate week-ends throughout the season. For those wishing to sail on Loweswater, Crummock Water and Buttermere, permission must first be obtained from the National Trust at Broadlands, Borrans Road, Ambleside (see events, page 69).

Wrestling

CUMBERLAND AND WESTMORLAND wrestling is one of the oldest traditional sports in the Lake Counties. Sports meetings which include this style of wrestling are held in many of the towns and villages throughout the area.

The contestants wear the traditional white stockings and gaily embroidered trunks, and each tries to throw his opponent to the ground. The champion is the wrestler who overthrows all the contestants at his weight. Anyone wishing to obtain more detailed information should write to the Cumberland and Westmorland Style Wrestling Association, 193, Brampton Road, Carlisle.

APRIL

Penrith
Acorn Bank, Temple Sowerby. The gardens are open from April
to September on three afternoons each week—Wednesday, Saturday
and Sunday. Of special interest are the daffodils in the spring, the
wide variety of summer flowers, and a herb garden which is being
developed. Admission is 10p.

Keswick
Lingholm Gardens are open to the public from April to October
every week-day except Sunday. These are large gardens especially
noted for rhododendrons and azaleas, woodland and exceptional
views of Borrowdale. Opening times are 10-5, and admission is 15p
for adults and 5p for children under the age of 12. Dogs on leads only.

Workington
Until recently the town was divided into two communities, a fact
celebrated at Easter when a football match is played in the streets
between the "uppies," the colliers of Curwen's new town, and the
"downies," the fishermen and shipwrights of the old town by the
marsh.

The hound trailing season begins in April, usually Easter week-end,
and trails are held throughout the summer in all parts of the Lake
Counties. Details may be found in the local press and are displayed
in local shops and post offices (see Sports and Hobbies, page 63).

MAY

Carlisle
The Carlisle area eliminating contest for the Lorry Driver of the
Year Competition is held at the Ministry of Transport Centre in
Kingstown Road. Drivers take their vehicles, varying from 20 cwt.
vans to tankers, some over 40 feet long, through a specially laid out
obstacle course before being sent on a road test through the city. The
winners from each section go forward to the national finals which
are held at Coventry in September.

Lake District Festival
The Festival is held every two years for two weeks at the beginning of May, alternating with the Mary Wakefield Music Festival. Beginning in 1960 with concerts in Kendal and Cartmel, it has since spread to many parts of the Lake District including Windermere, Ambleside, Keswick and Penrith. The principal features are concerts, but lectures and exhibitions are also held.

Penrith
Held at Pooley Bridge, Ullswater, the Sports and Gala Day is considered to be the first of the major Lakeland sports meetings. Events include traditional Lakeland sports, professional foot racing, cycle racing, fell races, hound trails and whippet racing.

Sowerby Row, Carlisle
Sowerby Row Pony Show and Gymkhana is a one-day event which includes hound trails, children's sports, a donkey derby, pony classes and horse jumping under B.S.J.A. rules. There is also a very old traditional contest for men and boys for "gurning through a baffin." The contestants place their head through a horse collar, and the one to pull the funniest face wins. This can also be seen at the Egremont Crab Fair in September, held in southern Lakeland.

Late May is the time to see the coast near Maryport, for the only hill of the region is covered with a carpet of bluebells.

Sheep dog trials are held in May at Cockermouth and Alston.

The opening meet of the Kendal and District Otter Hounds is usually held on the first Saturday in May at Milnthorpe. The pack is one of only two pure-bred packs in Britain and their territory extends from the river Ribble through the Lake District to the river Eden. The otters, though hunted, are not in fact killed, but the pack does hunt and kill wild mink.

JUNE

Abbey Town, Carlisle
A Festival of the Arts is held at Holm Cultram Abbey, Abbey Town, for three weeks during June. Events include drama, recitals, concerts and exhibitions. Refreshments are available. Further details may be obtained from the Festival Office, Abbey Town, Carlisle (see Holm Cultram Abbey, page 43).

Cockermouth
Gala Week includes many varied events of interest to all ages, with five-a-side football, drama, music, a cycling pursuit race, donkey derby, and a mile-and a-half raft race on the river Cocker, starting in Harris Park. A highlight is a procession of tableaux through the streets and the crowning of the Gala Queen.

Keswick
The Century Theatre, the only mobile theatre in Britain, is based at

Keswick during the summer season. The company present a programme of progressive theatre at various locations throughout the Lake Counties.

Maryport

A Gymkhana and Field Day is held at Netherland Park on the first Saturday in June. The programme includes pony showing, jumping competitions held under B.S.J.A. rules, a pet show with classes for dogs, cats, rabbits and other pets, troupe dancing and terrier racing.

The National Trust and the Ministry of Agriculture organise "Look Ins" on Lakeland farms during the summer. These show visitors how the Lakeland farmers work, and they will be able to compare fell farming with that carried on in the valleys. The farms are owned by the National Trust and the public are free to attend. Prior booking is unnecessary and the days are well advertised in advance.

JULY

Carlisle

The Cumberland Agricultural Show, held at Bitts Park, is the largest one-day agricultural show in Britain. Usually taking place on the third or fourth Thursday in July, it features cattle judging, horse jumping, a dog show, a section for rabbits and cavies and a large number of trade stands.

Cockermouth

The Cockermouth Agricultural Society stages a one-day show at Greenlands. There are classes for cattle, sheep, foxhounds, terriers, Shetland ponies and saddle horses. There are also jumping competitions held under B.S.J.A. rules and a large comprehensive industrial section which includes classes for children. Also of interest are hound trails and terrier racing.

Keswick

A Christian Convention, first held in 1875, takes place annually in Keswick for one week during July. Meetings and services are held daily and people of all ages and from many countries attend.

Lorton

The Melbreak Hunt Show and Trials take place at Cass Howe, Lorton, on the last Saturday in July. There are open foxhound and puppy classes from all packs, terriers entered and un-entered, hound trails, terrier racing and open sheep dog trials. Many of the events in the Lake Counties include classes for working terriers. Anyone wishing to obtain further information about the Fell and Moorland Working Terrier Club should contact the Secretary, 8 Brisco Road, Egremont, Cumberland.

Maryport

Carnival Week covers a varied programme, featuring an athletic meeting, a dog show, archery competitions, etc. The carnival parade includes a large number of tableaux and competition for prizes is keen. A carnival is also held at Flimby.

Skiddaw
The Lake District Mountain Trial Association organises an annual race involving the ascent and descent of Skiddaw. The start and finish are in the Lower Fitz Park, Keswick, and competitors follow the footpath around Latrigg (north side) and the main footpath to the top, 3,053 feet, returning the same way—a distance of approximately nine miles. Competitors must be amateurs and over 18 years of age. The fastest time recorded for the race is 63 minutes 5 seconds.

AUGUST

Armathwaite
On the Summer Bank Holiday Monday, sports are held mainly for children, and events include flat races for boys and girls, high jump, three legged races and sack races. During the programme of events three hound trails are held. Similar sports are also held at Dearham, which include a pony gymkhana.

Bassenthwaite
Sailing Week is the main event of the Bassenthwaite Sailing Club's open calendar. The meeting is open for G.P. 14, National 12 and International Cadet dinghies. Racing is held under the rules of the I.Y.R.U. and the R.Y.A. on each day throughout the week, and the event attracts visitors from all parts of the country.

Brampton
The Brampton and District Horticultural Society's annual show includes many classes for flowers, fruit and vegetables. There is a children's section, classes for floral art, and an industrial section.

Carlisle
The proclamation of Carlisle Great Fair is read from Carlisle Cross at 8 a.m. following a civic procession, on the 26th August. A charter was granted to the city in 1352 by Edward III for a fair to be held on the Feast of the Virgin's Assumption. Although Carlisle Fair is no longer held, the tradition of reading the proclamation still continues.

The Border Counties Hound Club Open Dog Show is held at the Market Hall. The Maryport and District Canine Association also hold a show in August.

Dalemain, near Penrith
This is the venue for the annual Fell Pony Society Breed Show. This is the largest show of fell ponies in Britain, and includes classes for in-hand, riding and driving. A feature of the show is a miniature cross country ride. As well as local Lakeland fell ponies, there are also entries from Wales, Devon, Cornwall and Scotland. Refreshments are available. Dalemain is on the Penrith to Ullswater road.

Dalston
A flower show takes place on the Summer Bank Holiday Monday
and features classes for both flowers and vegetables. The most
popular flower classes are for dahlias and chrysanthemums.
Keswick
An agricultural show and industrial exhibition is held in "The
Howrahs," Keswick, on the Summer Bank Holiday Monday. The
show is open from 10 a.m. and, as well as industrial exhibits, the
programme includes classes for fell ponies, driving turnouts, riding
ponies, sheepdogs, foxhounds and open jumping. There is a children's
dog show, gymkhana, wrestling and fell racing. Hound trails are
held during the afternoon. Admission is 25p for adults and 5p for
children. There are car parking facilities (15p).
Loweswater
The Melbreak Hunt holds an annual barbecue on the last Friday in
August (Bank Holiday) which is open to all.
Skelton
A horticultural and agricultural show is held in Uthank Park and
includes classes for cattle, sheep, and horses. Visitors to the show
can also see four hound trails, a gymkhana, show jumping and
whippet racing. This one-day show, set in beautiful parkland
surrounded by trees, commences at 10.30 a.m.
Temple Sowerby
A flower show includes amateur and open classes for fruit, flowers
and vegetables, as well as an industrial section and various children's
classes.
   Other flower and vegetable shows include Maryport, Bridgefoot,
Little Clifton and Chapel Brow, Great Clifton, Harrington.

SEPTEMBER

Carlisle
The two-day show of the Carlisle and Cumberland Horticultural
Association is held in the Market Hall, and includes flower, vegetable,
fruit, produce, industrial and wine classes. There is a section for
cage birds, mainly budgerigars and canaries. The floral art exhibits
are of special note.
Gilsland
The sheep show includes, as well as sheep dog trials, three hound
trails held under British Hound Trailing Association rules. There is
also a large industrial section.
Hesket Newmarket
An agricultural show with classes for ponies and light horses, local
sheep breeds, foxhounds and terriers is held in September. There is a
competition for horse driven turnouts, pony sports and junior
jumping competitions held under B.S.J.A. rules. In addition to
terrier racing there are also hound trails. Admission is 25p, car park

10p. Refreshments are available.
Other Agricultural Shows include Alston.

Slaggyford
Two-day sheep dog trials are held in September. The local trials are held during the afternoon of the first day, and the whole of the second day is for open trials.

Wigton
The Cumberland Foxhounds Branch of the Pony Club hold their hunter trials at Westward Park. These comprise a cross-country event and show jumping, and four classes covering competitors whose ages range from under 12 to over 18 years of age.

Workington
A drama festival is held at the Carnegie Theatre, which is sponsored by the Restoration Arts Theatre in conjunction with the Workington Public Library and Workington Arts Club.

A mountain trial is organised by the Lake District Mountain Trial Association on the second Sunday in September. The course is usually between eighteen to twenty miles in length and is considered to be one of the most arduous fell races in the country. The location is changed each year, but is widely advertised locally and in the press. Primarily an endurance and route finding test, the competitors have to carry map, compass, waterproof clothing and their own sustenance. As in orienteering the competitors are not given the route, only map references of the check points.

OCTOBER

Carlisle
An exhibition of local art is held at the City Art Gallery, Tullie House, for approximately four weeks.

Wigton
A horse sale is held on the last Wednesday in October, and is the largest one day horse sale in the country, often continuing until late evening. There are approximately seven hundred horses, ponies and donkeys for sale.

The first meets of the hunting season are held in October. (For further details of the various packs see Sports and Hobbies, page 63.) The opening meet of the Melbreak Foxhounds is held on the 2nd or 3rd Saturday at Kirkstile at 9.30 a.m. Other annual meets of the Melbreak include the Jobby's Hunt at Kirkstile and the Shepherds Meet at Buttermere in November, Boxing Day Meet at Lorton, and New Year's Day hunt at Kirkstile. The opening meet of the Blencathra Foxhounds is held at Salutation, the Boxing Day Meet at Keswick and the New Year's Day Meet at Mungrisdale.

INDEX